GIVING GOOD GIFTS

The Spiritual Journey of Parenthood

George E. Conway

Westminster John Knox Press
LOUISVILLE • LONDON

© 2001 George Conway

Scripture quotations, unless otherwise indicated, are from the New Revised Stan-dard Version of the Bible, copyright © 1989 by the Division of Christian Educa-tion of the National Council of the Churches of Christ in the U.S.A., and are used by permission.

Scripture quotations marked NJB are from *The New Jerusalem Bible,* copyright © 1985 by Darton, Longman & Todd, Ltd., and Doubleday, a division of Bantam Doubleday Dell Publishing Group, Inc. Reprinted by permission of the publishers.

Excerpts from Martin Luther King, Jr., "Love, Law and Civil Disobedience," *A Tes-tament of Hope: The Essential Writings of Martin Luther King, Jr.,* ed. Coretta Scott King (New York: Harper & Row, 1986), p. 48. All quotations, copyright Martin Luther King, Jr. Quotations renewed Coretta Scott King and the Heirs to the Estate.

For more information about this book, go to the www.givinggoodgifts.com Web site.

Book design by Sharon Adams
Cover design by Pam Poll Graphic Design
Cover illustration: © 2001 Stone

First edition
Published by Westminster John Knox Press
Louisville, Kentucky

This book is printed on acid-free paper that meets the American National Stan-dards Institute Z39.48 standard. ∞

PRINTED IN THE UNITED STATES OF AMERICA

04 05 06 07 08 09 10—10 9 8 7 6 5

Library of Congress Cataloging-in-Publication Data

Conway, George E.
  Giving Good Gifts: The Spiritual Journey of Parenthood /
  George E. Conway.—1st ed.
    p. cm.
  Includes index.
  ISBN 0-664-22563-2 (alk. paper)
    1. Children—Religious life. 2. Parenting—Religious aspects—Christianity.
    3. Religious education of children. I. Title.
  BV4526.2.C63 2001
  248.8'45—dc21   2001040506

To Peggy Conway Shedlock

CONTENTS

ACKNOWLEDGMENTS

*T*his book would not have been possible without the support of the St. Anne's-Belfield School Board of Trustees. Through the granting of a sabbatical and staff support, the board made it possible for me to keep the demanding schedule of head of school while completing this book. Thank you all for twenty wonderful years!

Thanks also to my dear friends, the Reverend Dr. Fred R. Anderson, senior minister of the Madison Avenue Presbyterian Church and the Reverend Dr. Thomas K. Tewell, senior minister of the Fifth Avenue Presbyterian Church, New York, for their support and guidance. Their invitations to speak helped me focus my thoughts more clearly, and I am grateful for their help and the intelligent responses of their congregations. Fred particularly helped me by carefully reading and critiquing this work. I don't know that I ever met his high standards, but it was fun trying! Thank you, Fred and Tom, for the encouragement! You are true princes of the Kirk.

A special thanks to Professor Diogenes Allen of Princeton Theological Seminary for encouraging me to write this book. He has been an important influence in my intellectual life.

My mother, my wife, and my daughter have each, in her own way, contributed to this work. My mother was the most important person in my life and is now with the Lord. Knowing my mother, heaven is even cleaner now than when she got there.

Deborah, my wife, lived with the mistress of this book for years. Summer vacations and our dream sabbatical in France were all organized around "the book." She has been long suffering, but she hasn't suffered in silence. "Stop talking about this stuff and write it" was her gentle, constant, but firm admonition.

Elizabeth, my daughter and the great joy of my life, must be singled out for all she has taught me. Thank you for letting me use you as an example of important points. I don't consider myself a great father, but I feel like one in your presence. She, like her mother, keeps me at once inspired and humbled. Once when visiting South Carolina, we came upon a Civil War memorial erected in honor of a fallen officer by his daughter. I commented about how nice it was for the soldier's daughter to honor her father in that way. I was too transparent. Sensing my fishing expedition, Elizabeth allowed that she too would erect a memorial to me, and inscribe it: *TO THE MAN WHO TRIED TO WRITE A BOOK.*

Our great family friend and colleague of mine, Diana Edwards Smith, deserves a special thanks. She has worked with me on many projects and has taught me so much about writing that words cannot convey my gratitude. She is, simply, the greatest teacher I have ever known. If anything inspiring, literate, or interesting is in this book, she taught me how to express it.

Thank you, Mike Waylett, Jane Perry, Sharon Ortiz, Mary Matter-Harris, and Scott Hultstrand. Your editorial help and attention to detail have made this work more enjoyable.

Finally, I am grateful to Vince Patton for believing in this project. You plucked me, like Saul, out of the baggage. Thank you for your confidence in me.

George E. Conway
Charlottesville, VA

Introduction

Train children in the right way,
and when old, they will not stray.
Proverbs 22:6

What will your children be like when they are adults? How will they respond to life's inevitable losses? Will they have the strength to grow and be transformed by suffering and tragedy or will they be embittered and beaten down? What spiritual food will help them to grow a mature faith, a faith strong enough to remain compassionate despite hardship?

And what will you be like when your children are grown? Will you simply be a little older and a little wiser about some things? Lonely, but perhaps relieved? Will you be faced with filling the void they have left in your life with work, hobbies, or other distractions? Or will you have been changed for the better? Will the experience of rearing a child have deepened you spiritually, propelled you along a spiritual journey of your own? Will you be closer to God because you touched a child's life? Remember, the Bible tells us that God could think of no better way to be revealed to us than to come into the world as a baby. And just like that child in Bethlehem, each child is a deeply spiritual being with a power to help us adults see new things.

The parent-child relationship is one of the most unique in all of life. The very presence of children in our lives seems to heighten our awareness of the spiritual dimension of life. Yet, paradoxically, the spiritual lives of these little ones depend on us for spiritual nurture. Just as they need our care to grow physically and mentally, they also need our help to grow spiritually. In return, children open transcendent possibilities in us; they can draw us beyond ourselves. This is what is so wonderful about being a parent: We and our children are changed by the gifts we give to each other.

To guide our parenting effort, most of us look back to our own experiences as children and to the way our parents reared us. Whether those are happy memories or not, most parents want to do a better job than their parents did. We want to rear our children "in the right way," as the psalmist says. The problem is, kids don't come with an operating manual. For help, particularly during difficult times, parents often turn to friends, psychologists, and even self-help books.

The advice parents receive from experts can be conflicting, depending on the values and experiences of those consulted. According to one researcher[1] who has written about the dilemma of modern parents, ultimately, parents find most modern child-rearing advice to be "shallow and fruitless." This is because too often, parenting advice ignores the spiritual side of a child's life as well as the spiritual dimension of parenting. Both of these aspects of the parent-child relationship are powerfully important. The lasting relationship between parent and child—the one that extends into adulthood—is formed by what a parent does to touch the soul of a child. In order to have a lasting relationship with a child that can grow from the dependency of the crib to natural friendship in maturity, a parent must address the spiritual needs of a child at each stage of life.

Scripture assures us that God knows our needs before we ask. We know we are at our best as parents when we can anticipate our children's real needs. Tiny babies can only cry to express themselves; we must figure out what they are trying to tell us. Even as children grow and communication becomes more sophisticated, often parents are still left wondering what children really need as opposed to what they say they want. We are often assured by experts that when the simple wonder of a young child turns into the narcissistic self-indulgence of early adolescence, this is only a phase in a child's development. This is not true. Children grow inward if they are not drawn beyond themselves. We wouldn't think of saying, "Oh, let's not buy any food this week. He can find it on his own." Yet many parents foolishly hope that a child's emotional resiliency will grow without feeding the child's spiritual hunger.

No church program, psychological theory, or parenting technique can substitute for a parent's concerted effort to nurture a child's budding spirituality. God knows how to do this and has shown us how. Discovering what we can learn from God about being a parent is the subject of this book.

Malnourished Generation

A lot of spiritual junk food is being served in our society. There are trite sayings and emphatic sentiments in books on spirituality that sound good but that are not connected to anything other than themselves. These are just pretty clouds that float on the horizon. Children need real spiritual roots. They need more than just an exploration of their own feelings. They need a connection to traditions that have stood the test of time. They will flourish when they are exposed to stories and ideas that are so big and so real that they can provide shelter during the emotional storms of life. I once heard a college chaplain complain, "What I see are young people who have been given such religious platitudes growing up that they can't incorporate real life into their faith."[2] This is the result of being fed only spiritual junk food as a child.

How do we give our children more than that? How do we give children a spiritual inheritance so that in a world of rampant consumerism, they grow into young people who are concerned about people less fortunate than they? How do we teach children that in a world of violence and self-destructive behavior, they should choose life; in a world in which they are told "everyone lies," they can hold fast to God's truth; and, in a world of cynicism, they can see God?

Much of the youth culture is not healthy. From the provocative way young girls are encouraged to dress and behave to the often pernicious music and video industry, our youth are surrounded by choices most of us didn't face until college. From the youngest age, sexually suggestive advertising surrounds our children, and each day, they see multiple acts of violence on television. It is sad, but not surprising, that many young people in our culture eagerly flirt with danger and death. Through aberrant behavior, experimentation with drugs, and sexual activity at ever-earlier ages, many young people are living by rules that seem bizarre even to their post-sexual-revolution-era parents.

Yet in sharp contrast to the prevailing culture of destruction, some youth don't seem to have the need to tempt death in order to find meaning in life. These youth choose to be positive even when many around them wallow in cynicism. It seems they have made a conscious decision to choose life even when many of their peers see no reason to value it.

Over my nearly thirty years in schools, I have worked with hundreds of young people and their families as a teacher, school administrator, chaplain, and coach. They have told me their stories and have helped me see some things that didn't seem obvious at first: These young people were growing a spiritual life as they were growing physically, mentally, and emotionally. They were on a journey like all youth, but they took each step with a predisposition to include the spiritual dimension of life in their decisions. That capacity allowed them the room to grow and to develop their own healthy spiritual identities.

Reflecting on these young people's stories and lives, I found the major factors that usually separate people into groups, such as socioeconomic status, race, intelligence, or religious heritage, didn't seem to matter. I have known youth with healthy spiritual identities who didn't even go to church more than others their age. Although most of my work has been in private schools, the spiritually grounded kids I have known came from a mixture of homes—some were from wealthy families, others were full-scholarship kids. Their gender didn't seem to matter, either. The outward features were indistinguishable, but there was clearly something different going on inside.

The youth who exhibited a true spiritual depth that seemed to guide their behavior as well as inform their choices were much like any others. As middle school students, they cringed just like their peers when their mothers gave them a hug in public. When they became high school students, they looked the same, and their problems sounded very much like everyone else's. What was different was that they went about finding solutions to their problems in healthier ways. I have given a great deal of thought to these young people, and the more I have reflected on them and their stories, the more I have begun to see something very different about them. No, they didn't have some sort of special spiritual intelligence. However, they all had received a special reservoir of inner strength from which they drew every day.

A real breakthrough for me came when I realized that this spiritual reservoir provided a godly grounding, and that this grounding was given to these young people by their parents. The effective parents I knew didn't necessarily have psychology degrees or theological training, but they all had taught their children eternal truths. As I have gotten to know these parents and listened to their children, it has become clear to me that these parents were often drawing on the examples of our divine parent to guide their parenting.

A friend in whom I confided some of my earliest ideas for this book asked a question that I have now heard, in different ways, from laypersons and clergy alike. I told her that I was going to write about how the way God had parented characters in the Bible could serve as a model for how we might be good parents to our children. She found that thesis curious: "Do you really think God is a good example to parents?" After all, she reasoned, God seems to be a cruel parent in the Bible. God punished Adam and Eve (and all their offspring) simply because they took a small bite of fruit. The testing of Job seems capricious at best. The demand that Abraham sacrifice his son as a sign of faithfulness and God's own act of sending Jesus as a sacrifice for the sins of the world suggested to her that although God might be a great God, God doesn't seem like a very good parent.

To understand the God of the Bible as a divine parent, I decided to listen to young people, not adults. From young people, I learned that stories such as the Genesis account of the serpent in the garden do not represent God's neglect and ultimate harsh judgment on unsuspecting children. Rather, they show God as a parent who loved children enough to give them the freedom to make mistakes and yet still loved them despite their failings. My students taught me that God gave these children more distance, just like good parents thoughtfully offer their children the first steps of real independence before they are asked. Many young people wish their parents acted more like God. We adults may see the biblical God as an angry and distant figure, but adolescents read about the relationship between God and Adam, or between Jesus and his earthly parents, and see their own struggles.

I have come to the simple conclusion that of all the parenting advice available, the most useful comes from the Bible. God's Word speaks to all of us from across the ages, and its power is in its ability to speak anew and personally to each of us, no matter our needs. It should not surprise us, then, that the Bible could be helpful to us as we try to foster the spiritual dimension of a child's life. The Bible is not a "how to" book, but by reflecting on some of the ways our God acted as a divine parent, we can learn constructive ways of parenting our children.

In the pages that follow, I describe seven gifts parents can give their children that will help their children develop healthy spiritual identities. I will show how, in giving these gifts to a child, we as parents are changed by the giving as much as the child is changed by receiving the gifts. Through searching Scripture for God's insights and by reflecting on some of the good and bad examples of parenting I have seen, we will find that parenting is not just a walk with our children into their adulthood. Rather, by incorporating what we can learn from God into our parenting, child rearing can be a life-changing experience that can deepen our own connection to God and change us and our children for the better.

Seven Spiritual Gifts

Chapter 1: The Companionship of God

As a teacher of the Bible, I have noticed that some young people read Scripture and see God, whereas others read just as intently and see only shadows, myths, and fairy tales. Some are eager to grow spiritually and are curious about matters of faith and religion, but others seem only self-absorbed and oblivious to these topics. What is the difference?

Children are born with an innate sense of wonder. You can see it in their eyes. This is the root of the capacity for faith in God. Unless that wonder is cultivated and that capacity is nurtured by the most meaningful adults in the child's life, it never develops. As I listened to those students for whom questions of faith had real meaning, I noticed that although they were very different from each other, they all had one thing in common: When they reached for examples from their lives to illustrate a point or to frame a question, very often they talked about their relationships with their parents.

These were young people tempted and distracted just like everyone else by all the confusing signals our society now gives. They faced dark moments in their lives, just like everyone their age. However, they went about finding answers to their questions and solutions to their problems in a very different way. If there is one thing most parents would change about their children's lives, it would be to be with them when they face their most difficult emotional challenges and greatest temptations. We think we could help our children by supporting them, sharing our insights, drawing upon our experience. Of course, we know we can't do that. Our children will face their most difficult moments and their greatest temptations when we are not around to help them. We can, however, give our children something far better than our overly protective presence. We will fulfill our spiritual obligation to our children if we help them create a spiritual reservoir in their lives, a capacity to see God that can be filled at some points and drawn upon during the most vulnerable times of their lives.

Ask teaching or counseling professionals who have been working with young people for a long time, and they will tell you that youth are into more dangerous behavior than ever. The drugs are stronger, and our culture is encouraging behavior in children previously reserved for consenting adults. Young, almost prepubescent boys and girls, are displayed in provocative positions of half-undress on the sides of city buses and on the covers of magazines. When I asked my students their opinions about the controversial Calvin Klein ads, which featured young boys and girls tugging on their designer jeans and tantalizingly displaying the tops of their underwear, my students laughed. They knew young people's bodies had been used to sell clothes for a long time, and they were amused that the adults were finally getting upset by it. It seems true, our kids are getting older, younger.

Curiously, however, youth don't seem very happy about it. Suicide is the third most frequent cause of death among this age group, and our children are more medicated than ever. If you throw in the categories of traffic accidents and deaths attributed to drug use (including alcohol), the number of children who are choosing death over life is staggering. At a time when life seems so full of possibilities, many of our children are tempting death. The youth we know as "Goths," those spike-haired children who crowd together at the mall in their black leather clothes and pierced body parts, are but the most visible symbol of a youth culture that glorifies the macabre. When you talk to them, they are not optimistic. It is as if they were given the ability to live, but not the gift of life.

Children cling to life when they have God in their lives. That sense of God's presence in their lives is the first step in a child's journey toward a mature relationship with God. Children are introduced to God's presence in life by their parents. There is simply nothing more important a parent does for a child. This first chapter explores how a parent can give this precious gift.

Chapter 2: Finding God

Recognizing that each child has the capacity to have a personal relationship with God and understanding our role in cultivating the child's spiritual identity are the first steps toward creating the spiritual reservoir children need. Once our children begin their own spiritual journey, they will draw on the next gift we give to them: the ability to see God in their daily lives.

The ability to see God should not be confused with a necessity for some sort of conversion experience or private epiphany. The capacity to see God in one's life is not the result of a successful completion of a catechism or even of confirmation into the life of the church. The sight to which I refer is more like "insight" into the true meaning of events that surround us every day. It is a perspective on life that can only be shaped by years of care. It takes time to develop children's spiritual eyesight, and it's sad when those who love them don't help them develop this fundamental spiritual skill.

I was once asked by two fifth-grade girls what I thought God looked like. I told them I didn't know, and that, in fact, no one does. I told them, however, that I know when I'm near to God. That got their attention. "How?" they blurted out. I told them something once told to me when I was their age: God is all around us, but we don't know where God is because we don't have magic glasses on (like the ones used to view 3D movies) that allow us to see God. The only way we can develop the special eyesight we need is to pray every day and spend some time reflecting on the day and the events, small and large, that comprised it. We need to ask ourselves, when did I feel closest to God today, and when did I feel farthest away? By reflecting on the events of daily life, one starts to "see" God by first feeling God's presence. It's like closing your eyes and walking toward a fire. You can feel when you are getting close and when you are getting farther away. Once you get some practice at this, you can find God and choose to move closer every day.

The girls said, almost like a Greek chorus, "How do you know that?" I said I learned it by studying the Bible, by going to church, and by listening to the lessons adults taught me as a child. Then one said a very sad thing. She asked if she could ever learn to feel God if no one ever taught her. "My parents don't take me to church. They say our family doesn't believe in God," she stated. It was clear that she wanted to see God, but her parents weren't giving her the nutrition she needed to grow good spiritual eyesight.

We don't have to have perfect spiritual eyesight ourselves in order to help our children. The stories of the Bible can give our children important hints they need. This second chapter explores what we can do as parents to help our children develop the insight they need to find God in their everyday lives. When they have this gift, they can add it to their spiritual reservoir. From us and the stories of Scripture, they will learn one simple truth: When we try to walk toward God, God will find us.

Chapter 3: A Transcendent Perspective

Our love for our children makes us vulnerable. Many parents are terrified about making a wrong choice for their children. How frequently we read about frantic parents going to some extraordinary means to get their child into the right preschool, as if all the good things in life flowed from this first educational setting. Many of us are afraid if we miss one step, our children will be headed for disaster. We are plagued by the conflicting feelings of wanting our children to be independent, but not wanting them to suffer or fall behind at any point.

Seeing things from God's perspective requires looking beyond the blinders our culture and our fears place on us. One does not achieve this long view of life, this transcendent perspective, just by wishing for it. This chapter's topic is how we can gain a true understanding of what really matters in life and the judgment to make the right decisions for our children. We start by looking at the life of Abraham. A man of monumental shortcomings, Abraham achieved a transcendent perspective on life, which allowed him to see things from God's perspective. Once he achieved this perspective, things changed in his life.

In this chapter, we will look at the story of Abraham the parent. Once we understand what God taught Abraham about being a parent, it will change our parenting.

Chapter 4: Truth: The Absolute Horizon

The horizon is where the earth meets the sky. The spiritual dimension of life is lived where God touches our life. Being able to see these points gives us a view of an absolute horizon, a reliable marker for life's journey. Once we locate those intersections in our lives, all that remains is to find the courage to walk toward them.

I was once challenged by an angry parent after I had detailed the events of an incident that resulted in his child being disciplined by the school. During my account, the father interrupted me at several points to assure me that the events did not happen as I described them. Unlike the angry father, I was present for the events, so I could guarantee him I was recounting the truth. In a final moment of frustration, he shouted at me: "That's your truth!"

In our culture, truth has become synonymous with mere opinion. A young alumnus recently told me of his dismay over the restraints on speech in his college classrooms. He said, "Any statement of conviction is criticized as imposing one's personal beliefs on others." He found this curious. He didn't see any "invisible hand" in his class discussions pushing ideas on helpless victims. Nevertheless, he was cautioned about sharing his beliefs. It seems our young people are being taught that they are only free from conviction, not truly free to hold convictions. In contrast, the Bible speaks of a timeless truth that offers an absolute horizon, a reliable moral compass that can be a starting point for all our decisions. To navigate the uncertain waters of our culture, children need this fourth gift added to their spiritual reservoir: the gift of a moral compass and sense of absolute truth.

Chapter 5: The Freedom to Doubt

There are those who believe that their interpretation of God's truth is the only interpretation. These are dangerous people, because their myopic vision of Scripture devolves God's message into a cult. It is the truth of the Bible that makes us free—free to have questions, and free to take our own path toward God. Parents must know how to help children grow an independent faith that is based on solid biblical truths. We must also prepare our children to encounter those who want to cloud the absolute horizon of God's truth with their self-serving version of what is right.

Good parents encourage their children to explore their doubts and test their beliefs. Christian faith gets stronger when it is forged in the hot oven of doubt. The first step toward this understanding is to help our children know that Christian doubt is different from self-doubt. The exercise of

Christian doubt draws us closer to God because it is a catalyst for deepening our faith. Belief not molded this way can become merely emphatic sentiment and doctrinal recitation.

It should be a great cause for concern to anyone who cares about kids or the intellectual traditions of mainstream Christianity that the fastest growing branch of our faith among young people is what can be described as 'easy answer' Christianity, a faith which does not allow for doubt. Often this myopic faith is promoted by evangelical fundamentalists. We must be fair: not all evangelical Christians promote this kind of narrow-minded belief structure propagated by some campus crusaders. Yet parents should be clear about the dangers present in the groups that want to enclose our children behind the walls of their narrow perspective on Scripture and encourage young people not to question. Any so-called religious tradition which requires conspicuous exhibition of prescribed behavior while stifling doubt is poisonous to young people. Our children should learn from us that the God of the Bible is a big God; God is not afraid of our doubts. Fortunately, Scripture can help us and help them to find ways of transforming doubts into a profound and resiliently mature faith.

This chapter explores the distinction between the message of mainstream Christianity and the so-called Christian right. The threat to our children, however, is not only from the extreme religious right; the schools to which we send them are often in the grip of a destructive cynicism. To help parents recognize the dangers our children encounter, this chapter explores the biblical teaching on doubt, and how we and our children may go about ferreting out God's truth in a culture that assaults it from both extremes.

Chapter 6: To Give Honor

Although honor is an old-fashioned word that sounds particularly anachronistic in our age, the Commandments of God require us to honor our parents. Why didn't God tell us to love our parents? The answer is important; for in the gift of honor we give our children, we can find a guide for everything we do toward our own parents.

Chapter 7: The Triumph of *Timshel*

Steinbeck tells us that *Timshel* is a derivative of a Hebrew phrase. It captures the biblical teaching that within us is a good greater than any evil the world can throw at us. An indispensable ingredient in a spiritually healthy individual is a reservoir of spiritual confidence so that we have, at our disposal, the power to overcome evil.

One of the most troubling aspects of the youth culture is its strange preoccupation with the dark side of life. Evil, devil worship, and Satanism all hold a sick fascination for many youth today. Even one of the most popular television shows, which features "professional" wrestling, has the constant subtheme of powerful menacing forces giving certain wrestlers extra powers.

We should worry about this phenomena and the other troubling manifestations of a culture that glorifies the macabre. However, we shouldn't fear them, because the Bible tells us we can have power over evil.

We know that all children struggle for control over their lives; that is part of growing up. Adult behavior is imitated by little children wearing daddy's shoes to ten-year-olds smoking cigarettes. The shoes aren't comfortable, and the cigarettes don't taste good. However, children and adolescents engage in what they perceive as adult behavior in order to share some of the power we adults seem to have over our lives. One of the consequences of a culture that has made truth relative and God's truth a matter of opinion is that evil has no foil. While the liberal churches have been psychologizing evil and Hollywood has been glorifying it, our children have been becoming more confused.

Timshel is a spiritual gift we can give to children, a gift emerging from Scripture that can give them ultimate power over the real evil in our world. Children are eager for this gift. Remember that when Luke Skywalker called on "The Force" and his light sabre sprang to life and gave him the power to fight evil, young audiences cheered. All children want that kind of weapon against evil—they want something to cheer about. In this chapter, we explore the Bible's insights into what we can tell our children about evil and into how we can help ignite God's power within them.

The Spiritual Journey of Parenthood

This final chapter is about us. Being a parent is a powerful experience, but we often don't anticipate the many ways it will change us. The concluding chapter is a discussion about how parents can deepen their spiritual lives by allowing child rearing to create a special spiritual journey of its own. In it, we will explore such questions as: How can we grow through our occasional ambivalent feelings about being a parent? What do we do when we feel anger toward our children? Anger and ambivalence plague every parent from time to time, even God. Through the stories preserved for us in the Bible, we will learn how these feelings can actually be a catalyst for spiritual growth.

Giving spiritual gifts to our children starts us on the spiritual journey of parenting. So, I end this book with some thoughts about how we might become spiritual mentors to our children. Before we can help them, however, we must help ourselves. It is like the advice we get from the flight attendants who instruct us that we must first put on our oxygen masks before we help the children traveling with us. When we cultivate our spiritual center as parents, we are preparing to help our children develop theirs. When we tap into God's power, our parenting draws us closer to God, closer to our children, and even closer to the best parts of ourselves.

Chapter 1

The Companionship of God

*S*everal years ago, a middle school student at my school shot and killed himself. As far as I know, it has never been officially determined whether his act was intentional or simply tragically careless. He left no note. As he had most every evening of his life, the night he died he shared dinner with his parents and grandparents. It should have been a good evening together. School had just ended, and the summer stretched before him. That meant plenty of time to do what he loved: work on the farm with his grandfather. The boy and his parents lived on his grandparents' farm, a bucolic setting. Over the years, the boy had formed a close relationship with his grandfather. Together they hunted, fished, and farmed. They were friends. But that night there was some disquieting news.

The boy's mother had received a call from the school earlier in the day. After a careful assessment of his work for the year, the faculty had recommended that he attend summer school. His mother had known this was a possibility, and so did he. And he, like any boy his age, hated the idea. She told him about the call just before they walked the short distance to his grandparents' house for their evening meal.

After supper, the boy left the table as the plates were being cleared before dessert and walked to his house. There he took one of the several guns to which he had easy access, guns his grandfather had taught him to respect and to handle with care, and killed himself.

Although school was out, the news of the tragedy quickly spread. Grief was deeply evident in every student, parent, and teacher who stopped by school in the days following the death. Among middle school students, a rumor circulated that the boy had killed himself because of his poor grades. Although that theory might sound preposterous on the surface, all of us who have worked with this age group know that lives have been taken for less than that.

I went to the family's home because I wanted the family to know that they were in the prayers of the entire school community. I hoped that this knowledge would bring them some comfort.

A friend of mine, who knew the family well, accompanied me on my visit. We were greeted at the door by the grandmother, a gentle yet commanding woman, who carried herself as do many prominent women of her generation. Relieved by her warmth and composure, I immediately began the conversation by expressing our condolences and asked if we might speak with the boy's parents. The grandmother graciously accepted our sympathy and thanked us for coming. She told us her daughter and her husband were upstairs; she seated us in the parlor and excused herself to get them. After a few minutes, she returned to tell us that they could not come downstairs just then, but that they appreciated our call. We said that we understood and were about to leave when suddenly the grandfather entered the room. I knew who he was because my friend greeted him by name. He acknowledged me coolly and, before I could finish expressing my sympathy, he interrupted me. "I should never have allowed my grandson to go to your school," he said angrily. "It was too much pressure on him. He couldn't do the work. I want you to know, Dr. Conway, that I hold you and your school responsible for my grandson's death, and I want to know what you are going to do about it."

His wife, who stepped to his side, whispered something too softly to convey anything other than sadness and embarrassment. The intensity of the old man's anger and pain left me speechless. All I could say was, "I'm sorry."

My friend, who was also a member of the school's Board of Trustees, tried to help by expressing the sympathy of the Board and everyone associated with the school. But the man would hear none of it. He simply left the room. I think I exhaled then for the first time since he had entered.

Outside, the boy's grandmother apologized for her husband's words. She hoped we would understand how difficult her grandson's death had been on everyone. We did. We drove off the farm, but several hundred yards down the road, I pulled over. My friend and I just sat there for a while and tried to recover from the experience.

At the funeral, I spoke to the grandparents and parents at the grave site. All were cordial and composed but obviously distraught. They seemed pleased that so many of the boy's teachers and fellow students were in attendance, but they didn't show any sign of being comforted by our presence. I left the grave sick to my stomach.

The grandfather's words have never left me. As a clergyman, I have grown accustomed to otherwise faithful people expressing their anger at

God's act of taking away a loved one. However, I had never before been held responsible for someone else's loss.

The longer his words haunted me, the angrier I got. "Why didn't *you* keep your guns locked safely away?" I imagined responding. "Why did *you* raise a grandson whose world was so fragile that he threw away his life just on the news of a few weeks of summer school?" I usually regret when I am speechless, but not that time. If I had actually said any of those imagined angry retorts to the old man, I never would have forgiven myself. The depth of his grief left me speechless, and I am glad I was silent.

As inconceivable as it may be to adults, otherwise healthy adolescents, young people who are loved and well cared for, have moments when they see little reason to live. Some blame television for this. The tube makes life seem so easy. So, when life isn't easy for our pampered children, they over-react. They strike out in frustration, sometimes hurting themselves, some-times hurting others.

Some social scientists think the desperation that occasionally over-whelms a young person is a sad confluence of erupting hormones that result in mercurial emotional swings. Sometimes these swings dangerously deepen a tendency in this age group to see their options with shortsighted absolutism. The result can be a dark gravity and overshadowing feeling that there is "no way out."

I don't know if either of these theories is right. I don't even know what really happened that night to my young student. Perhaps the boy's grand-father was right. Pressures at school had overwhelmed his grandson, and death seemed the only way out of his misery that the boy could see. But is it really possible that an otherwise healthy young person would kill him-self over the prospect of summer school?

As I noted earlier, suicide is the third most frequent cause of death among teenagers,[1] who, ironically, are members of the most medicated generation in history. Traffic accidents and deaths attributed to drug use (including alcohol), raise the number of children who are choosing death over life to staggering proportions. Those are just the hard statistics; what is just as disconcerting, however, is how many more suicide attempts are made each year by this age group. It is clear we have many children in our society who are profoundly unhappy and given to desperate acts to resolve their internal conflicts. What is not clear is why this is so.

A popular collection of "inspirational" stories for young people called *Chicken Soup for the Teenage Soul*[2] is now in its third volume. Page after page of this collection documents contemporary adolescent angst. Issues of dating, friendship, untimely death, and attempts to find meaning in one's life are told in heart-wrenching bromides. These stories are moving but not satisfying. They explore emotions but rarely point to anything beyond simple sentiment.

One anonymous *Chicken Soup* submission recounts how a despondent teenage girl was saved from suicide by a timely telephone call from a friend. It wasn't until the girl heard the friendly voice on the answering machine, as she stood in the basement with a gun to her head, that she realized someone loved her. By the way, the only reason given in the story for this potentially deadly act is that the suicidal girl was soon going to move to another part of town.

To the adult, this story might elicit the silent headshaking we do when we hear about some new senseless tragedy involving young people. However, the thousands of young people who have read these books find solace in these stories. Why does the *Chicken Soup* collection mean so much to young people? Could it be they are just settling for the little spiritual nourishment offered?

Suicide and other self-destructive and violent behavior in our society, including drug use and sexual promiscuity, have been receiving a great deal of attention from the research and psychiatric communities. Clever national advertising campaigns have been fashioned to try to prevent such life-threatening activities as binge drinking, drug use, and dangerous sexual behavior. What is it about our youth today that requires us to convince them not to hurt themselves?

Some destructive behavior in young people has been attributed to physiological conditions. Findings about the biological roots of behavior have led to chemical therapies for depressive disorders. This research has been helpful in treating those children who are depressed and whose depression we catch before they harm themselves or others. However, I don't believe all self-destructive or desperately violent behavior in young people is the result of emotional or chemical imbalance.

In talking with young people, observing their behavior, and following the research on the question of youth anger and depression, I have grown convinced that many youth turn against themselves and others because they are fundamentally malnourished. They are not neglected in outward ways; in fact, many come from privileged homes and attend safe schools. However, some youth hurt themselves or turn undifferentiated anger toward others, not because something is wrong with them, but rather because they lack spiritual depth and thus an emotional anchor in life. When confusion strikes, they strike out; sometimes they hurt themselves, sometimes others.

Some young people turn to violence because they suffer from a withered soul. Children need substantive spiritual sustenance for their souls just like they need dietary nourishment for healthy physical and mental growth. They need hope they can rely on, a certainty that springs from divine truth—not conditional statements that will seem like a dated hairdo when these youth look back upon their childhood. Compared to the hearty spiritual diet fed to children in the past, our children are being nourished only by chicken soup.

For former generations, faith formed the foundation of emotional resilience. Classic literature reflects a common understanding of past generations that seems absent from the lives of many of our children today. Edmond Dantes, for example, who later becomes the *Count of Monte Cristo*, lies in the bowels of the dreaded Chateau d'If, falsely accused by the Crown of being a Bonapartist. Edmond's beloved Mercedes contemplates suicide as a way of escaping her grief. She has good cause for inconsolable grief, at least by the standards by which young people judge such things. Her fiancé was arrested at their engagement feast and unjustly accused of a political crime. The authorities won't even tell her where he is, and she can only assume the worst. She has no hope of his return. She falls into utter despair, and her life, as she had envisioned it, is ruined. Alexander Dumas writes that she would have killed herself but did not because of "her religion."[3] That simple statement reveals a great deal about the assumption of his age; they believed that faith in God sustained life. At the dawn of the twenty-first century, one might be tempted to dismiss Mercedes' crisis as fictional hyperbole. But doing so would be a mistake.

Modern science now supports what writers like Dumas knew. In a fascinating book, Dale A. Matthews, M.D. documents the influence of what he calls the "faith factor"[4] through dozens of scientific studies. Study after study confirms that people who go to church and who profess faith in God live longer, happier lives. Perhaps most important, especially for parents, is that the suicide rate among churchgoers and people of faith is lower than the national average. It is clear to researchers that there is a palpable divine presence in our life and an abiding sense of hope when we believe in God. That belief translates into a personal relationship with the Deity. When God is in one's life, when the innate human capacity for faith in God grows into a sense of companionship with God, a miraculous power begins to work. It is powerful enough to save the life of a child by giving that child a strength to carry on when there seems to be no reason. It can give a child courage to struggle on against fears and feelings of isolation. The companionship of God is so powerful that sometimes merely being in its presence is enough to change a life. We know it changed one young man's life.

Justin's Story

Some call it taking time to "find yourself." Justin didn't know what he wanted to be when he grew up, but, by the world's standards, he was already grown up. Although in his early twenties, he still hadn't made up his mind about a profession. He wasn't married. He didn't even have a job. He felt he needed more time before he began all that—time to think, to read, and to talk out the great questions of life. Even as a boy, he had been fascinated with ideas of philosophy and knew if he just trained his mind properly, he could gain the insight he wanted and find the contentment that eluded him. He wanted to study with some of the great teachers and to explore his own nascent ideas. Perhaps he would write someday, be a scholar. He was not lazy, nor was he looking for a way to escape responsibility; he just had a profoundly restless spirit and an emptiness that gnawed at him. His father encouraged young Justin to continue his studies until he found what he was looking for—whatever that was, whenever that came.

Justin went to the big city where there were lots of young people, lots of excitement, and lots of interesting things going on. Soon after he arrived, he fell in with a group of fellow students, became friends with them, and enjoyed the good conversations and good times that followed.

When the holidays came, Justin's friends decided their friend needed a break from his studies. They decided it was time for this serious young man from the provinces to see the hottest show in town. Justin's friends had been drawn to him because of his gentleness and seriousness, but they also knew Justin had his head in the clouds; they agreed that a little reality would be good for him.

They were right. Justin had never seen anything like this. As he entered the stadium, his initial horror turned to fascination, and the excitement of the crowd and the power of the players mixed to make the whole experience intoxicating. The year was about 140 A.D., and the city was Rome.[5] At the Colosseum, Justin and his friends attended the great gladiatorial fights. The special occasion was Caesar's birthday.

The crowd cheered as these giant men fought with reckless abandon. The roar of the crowd was thunderous as the blows were struck and the blood flowed. Then came the moment of death, and the crowd grew silent. The defeated warrior, disarmed by his opponent, stretched out his neck to bravely receive the victor's final blow. Some in the crowd looked away. The whole stadium erupted in a single shout of approval when the winner raised his arms victoriously over his fallen opponent. With luck, the loser died a quick, merciful, and honorable death.

The coward, however, died a thousand times. If the unarmed took to his heels in the hope of reaching safety instead of facing his opponent's final blow, the crowd jeered at him, threw whatever they could find, and kept the helpless loser from climbing out of the pit to safety. Sometimes he succeeded, but most times he died anyway.

The crowd's appetite for bloodshed always exceeded the number of available gladiators. The show was not over when the last combatant fell. After all, this was the Emperor's birthday. So, to continue to please the audience, groups of unarmed, mostly illiterate people, men with their wives and children at their sides, were led into the arena to be torn apart by wild beasts who had been starved and crazed for the occasion. These doomed and pathetic people were a despicable lot. The Roman Senator Tacitus referred to them as "a class of people hated for their superstitions." They were the followers of "Christos," who had himself been crucified at the direction of Pontius Pilate about one hundred years earlier.

It may be that two men's lives were changed that day. We know of a Carthaginian prison guard who was in charge of these wretched people and who marveled at their faith. His job was to ensure the beasts were ready for their feast. We know he began to inquire about what these Christians believed during the long nights before they were to give their lives for entertainment. He envied their courage and, as a warrior, he knew the value of courage. We don't know the guard's name, but we know from the annals of the day that the guard, in time, became a Christian himself.[6]

The guard responded to the courage that the Christians showed in the face of an unimaginable death, but Justin marveled at the peace he saw in their eyes. As he watched these people, Justin realized that his quest had been about more than ideas. Justin had thought he was looking for the perfect argument leading to intellectual insight. That day he understood that he really had been looking for God. Justin saw in those people the power of life lived with God. In their silent courage, he knew he had seen a miracle.

The raw show of courage that these Christians displayed was a life-changing experience for him and the guard. We know nothing about where that guard's new faith took him. We do know from Justin's own writings that shortly after this experience at the gladiatorial stadium he met an old man who became a sort of spiritual guide to him, helping the young man to understand the Christian message he had seen alive in the defiant peace of those people.

Justin is more commonly known as Justin Martyr because he became a Christian during the dark days of the church's persecution in Rome, and he, too, was killed for his beliefs. He became a powerful preacher of the

Gospel and a major figure in the early Christian Church. Consequently, he became a threat to Rome. The record of his trial for being a member of the outlawed Christian sect details the terrible price he paid for his faith. During the time of Emperor Marcus Aurelius, Rusticus, a "despicable prefect of Rome," interrogated Justin. To Rusticus' questions about his beliefs, Justin replied with virtually the exact words Martin Luther would use in reply to his accusers nearly fifteen centuries later:

> I found this great faith the truest: here I take my stand. . . . Then the accursed magistrate ordered them (it was a group trial) to be chastised with whips. And they were scourged until their flesh was torn to shreds, and their blood reddened the ground. When he saw that the martyrs would in no wise yield, he gave sentence against them as follows: "I decree that those who have defied the imperial edicts and have refused to sacrifice to the gods are to be beheaded with the sword.[7]

Of Justin it is said that with the acceptance of the Christian faith, "the clouds broke, and he saw yet farther."[8] What Justin saw in the martyrdom of those simple people was a power greater than Rome's. He saw the strength that comes to those who know the companionship of God.

The image of the Son of God unjustly accused, yet sentenced to the cross, has inspired people throughout history to endure unspeakable persecutions. This idea of the weak victim, overcoming a powerful oppressor or a crushing set of circumstances through faith in God comes from the Bible; but, unfortunately, many of our young people are biblically illiterate and don't know these inspirational stories. They haven't heard about the characters whose faith enabled them to triumph over real adversity. For example, they don't know about Joseph, whose story taught hundreds of generations of young people that they don't have to give up if they walk with God.

Like Mercedes in the *Court of Monte Cristo*, Joseph had good cause for despair. His brothers hated him and sold him into slavery. As if that weren't enough, he was falsely accused of molesting a prominent man's wife and was cast into an Egyptian prison. There he languished. Spared only by his power to interpret dreams, he was eventually freed. Undaunted by his misfortunes, he rose to the second most powerful position of authority in Egypt. When circumstances later brought him face-to-face with his brothers, we assume that he must have hated them. However, instead of getting even, Joseph told them not to fear because, "even though you intended to do harm to me, God intended it for good" (Gen. 50:20). Reflecting on Joseph's kind of insight, Paul later wrote, "We know that all things work together for good for those who love God" (Romans 8:28). Sadly, many of our young people don't know these stories; they haven't been reassured that God's hand is always at work in their lives. They haven't experienced the companionship of God. Without that knowledge and that experience, despair is always close at hand.

Where Did Joseph Get His Faith?

You might be surprised to learn that Joseph got his faith from his father, Jacob. Jacob, in turn, was introduced to the companionship of God by his father. In fact, Jacob referred to the biblical Yahweh as "The God of my Father." This makes sense when you remember that only the first patriarchs spoke directly to God; thereafter, faith was a legacy passed down from parents to children. It was that faith, a gift from their parents, that sustained both Jacob and Joseph through their darkest hours. In Joseph's case, he had been given special abilities by God; he could interpret dreams. But it was his father's encouragement that eventually allowed Joseph to grow his own faith in God, one which not only gave him a reason to go on living through dark moments, but which gave him the power to forgive.

Our children deserve an inheritance like that, a spiritual reservoir to draw upon. The gift of religion to Mercedes, the faith Jacob gave to Joseph, and the encouragement by Justin's father, set them all on a path toward a life-sustaining spiritual identity. The companionship of God gave them something their peers didn't have: a reason to live when there seemed to be none. Bible teacher and psychologist Naomi Rosenblatt puts it this way:

> The belief that we are created in God's image acknowledges that we humans are blessed with attributes that separate us from the purely instinct-driven creatures on earth: free will, imagination, creativity, compassion, conscience, self-awareness, and a sense of the future.[9]

Without the companionship of God, it can be difficult for some young people to believe they have a future at all. The Bible teaches us in the first pages of Genesis that the connection between faith and future is built on the acceptance of one simple notion: We are made in the image of God. From that idea flows concrete for the footings of faith.

To explore the richness of this idea, we don't have to start from scratch on our own. Others—in fact, some of the greatest Christian thinkers of all time—have paved the way for us. To help us help our children, we can draw on their wisdom as well as on the insight of those whose faith may be simple but whose insight is profound.

Imago Dei

In classical theology, the importance of one's personal identity being connected to the belief that we are made in God's image was referred to as *imago Dei* [î-mâ-go day-e], Latin for the "image of God." This idea was so fundamental to understanding who we are and what our relationship with God is that it is raised in the very first chapter of the Bible. From there, it became the central assumption of all of Scripture.

> *Then God said, "Let us make humankind in our image,*
> *according to our likeness."*
>
> (Gen. 1:26)

The Bible tells us that when God created human life, God left a divine image upon us. However, how this *imago* is manifested in us and why it is so important are left for us to figure out.

Since the dawn of the modern age, psychology, sociology, and politics have dominated our understanding of who we are. But before the age of psychology, it was the biblical teaching that humans are somehow especially connected to our Creator through God's act of creation that dominated scholarly reflections on the meaning of human life.

St. Paul believed that the image of God was specifically and uniquely in Christ. Paul wrote in Colossians 1:15: "He [Jesus] is the image of the invisible God, the firstborn of all creation" (see also 2 Cor. 4:4). Therefore, it was our personal relationship with Jesus that made it possible for us to achieve true godliness and reflect the *imago Dei*. Paul's teaching forms the foundation of all Christian theology. His theology was what we call "Christocentric" because it put Jesus at the center of faith. Paul believed that the companionship of God was accessible to all through the acceptance of Jesus as our Lord and Savior and the reflection of Jesus' image through the acts of our lives.

Others writing about the same time as Paul did not see Jesus in the Genesis text. For example, Philo,[10] a Jewish Alexandrian philosopher who lived between 30 B.C. and 45 A.D., believed that it was our ability to feel God's presence in our lives that constituted our innate spiritual connection with God. This spiritual connection was in all people. In each of us was an indelible imprint left by God; a kind of pattern on our soul. All we had to do was connect with the image of God within us and we could grow closer to God. Philo turned the human search for companionship with God inward, while Paul pointed us upward toward Jesus.

The first prominent Christian theologian after Paul to discuss this matter was the second-century theologian and French churchman, Irenaeus. He was struck by both Paul's and Philo's ideas but saw an important distinction within verse 26 between "image"and "likeness."[11] He concluded that after Eden, we continued to bear the physical image of God somehow in our human composition, but the unique relationship between creature and creator, the spiritual link to God that made us godly, was broken through Adam's disobedience. For Irenaeus, this broken relationship accounted for our feelings of being estranged from God and creation. Irenaeus's work elaborated on the idea that Jesus Christ is the mediator between us and God. For him, it was the reuniting of image and likeness of God within us that was the work of the grace of God in Jesus Christ.[12]

A further development in the exploration of the meaning of the *imago Dei* came from one of the most important figures in theology. Known to us as St. Augustine, he was bishop in what is present-day Algeria from 396–430 A.D. and is considered by many to be the real founder of theology. Augustine introduced the idea that in Genesis 1:26, the "us" may refer not just to Jesus (as Paul had thought), but to the presence of the Trinity (Father, Son, and Holy Spirit) at creation. Drawing on Greek philosophy, Augustine believed that there were "three spiritual powers"[13] at work in the creation of human beings. These three powers, *memoria* (memory), *intellectus* (knowledge), and *amor* (love) were imprinted on man and woman at creation. These three unique powers together composed the *imago Dei* in us. They gave human beings the means to get back to God through the use of our intellect and faith, despite our sinful nature. For Augustine, the image of God gave us the human potential to be godly.

For centuries, Augustine's ideas had a profound effect on human self-understanding. His teaching nicely combined Paul's ideas with the fundamental precepts of Greek philosophy. The combination of biblically sound teaching and platonic philosophy made Augustine's interpretation the dominant theological thinking on this matter well into the seventeenth century.

There have been other, less successful attempts to interpret the "us" in Genesis 1:26. Some contemporary theologians have promoted the idea that the "us" was a reference to the motherhood as well as the fatherhood of God. This position suggested that God was androgynous, both male and female at creation. These ideas are not new. Attempts to make the Heavenly Father of the Bible androgynous have a long history and have resulted in some curiously counterintuitive statements like the one by the Church Council of Toledo in 675 A.D., which proclaimed that the Son of God was created, "out of the womb—uterus—of the

Father."[14] These ideas have not received wide acceptance among serious theologians.

The most profound blend of sound biblical scholarship and modern psychological understanding on Genesis 1:26 came from the twentieth-century theologian Karl Barth.[15] Barth contends that at the moment of creation, God was complete, but through this loving act, God gave a part of Himself to the man and woman.[16] From that moment on, God has desired to be reunited with human beings, and we yearn for a return to oneness with God. This fundamental desire for a sense of wholeness drives us spiritually toward God. This is what Isaiah referred to when he wrote, "My soul yearns for you in the night, my spirit within me earnestly seeks you" (Isa. 26:9).

Despite the fact that some of the greatest theological minds in history have reflected on the meaning of the *imago Dei*, there has been no enduring consensus on what the Genesis writer had in mind. It was, however, one of my young students who captured for me the best combination of the thinking of these great theologians. He spoke up during class while we were discussing the creation accounts in the first and second chapters of Genesis. "Maybe God puts it this way, 'let us make a person in *our* image,'" he offered, "because God wanted people to be thinking about Him before they thought about having a baby. After all, to a child, parents are like God."

I remember well how his face reddened with embarrassment after he made the comment and how he sank deeper into his seat. I instantly felt sorry for the boy. In the eyes of his peers, he had committed an unforgivable adolescent *faux pas*. Bravado led immediately to others in the class offering possibilities of what people are thinking when they are creating a baby! But I knew he had hit on something important.

His idea was simple, but compelling. God's gift of free will allowed us the freedom to just have sex, or to lovingly engage in the ultimate act of intimacy for the purpose of bringing another life into this world. Sexual intercourse then could be more than a physical act. This was a boy who had begun thinking about intimacy in a way that would lead him to responsible behavior. He would not have to be sensitized to his partner's feelings or reminded to adhere to safe sex practices. Although sex seemed to be at once sensationalized and trivialized in our culture, this young man sensed that something more important than just physical gratification was going on in the union of man and woman. The idea of the image of God was shaping his thinking, and his thinking would ultimately shape his behavior. This could have been what St. Paul had in mind when he encouraged the Ephesians to become "imitators of God" (Eph. 5:1).

Who gave my student the idea that being made in the image of God should affect his values and behavior? As I grew to know him, I found out. The simple faith of a loving parent was a seed now growing within him. Was this how Joseph got his strength? Was this what Mercedes got from "her religion"? Is that what Justin's father gave to his restless son?

Psychologists have taught us about the emotional importance of that first nurturing relationships between parent and child. There is a spiritual dimension to that relationship as well. The fundamental yearning that leads us to seek God is already in our children when they come to us. But that is just the start. It is our obligation to cultivate that yearning by giving it shape. Perhaps that explains why some of my students over the years, when they have a chance to study the Bible in a serious way, read Scripture and see God, whereas others are simply baffled by the book. Some young people already feel the imprint of God upon them, because as children their hands were guided by adult hands to feel the imprint of God on their hearts as Philo described. These young people can see God in the stories of the Bible and in life around them because the way has been paved by their parents.

When you teach these special young people, it is clear they sense the companionship of God. These children have been blessed with parents and other significant adults who have told them that they are here for something more than just to be units of consumption in a land of conspicuous consumption. In class and in conversations with them, they thread into their comments the idea that they are here for a higher purpose, and they develop their arguments based on this premise. They respect life, because they have a deep abiding sense that they are linked to all living things by their relationship to God. This is not mere egalitarianism or environmentalism, this is a sense that because they have a divine companion in life, they are linked to everything God made.

You might ask: Are you serious!? Are you suggesting that one of the reasons the young people who appear normal, but who suddenly and unexpectedly kill themselves, or who engage in life-threatening behavior that harms them or others, do so because they do not have a relationship with God?!

Yes. Youth who have been introduced to the companionship of God, who don't base their self-worth only on what others think of them, but rather on what God thinks of them, have a solid foundation on which to stand. Their world doesn't come unraveled very easily.

When the capacity for faith in God is not properly nurtured, young people may have little to hold them together in their most desperate moments. They can hurt themselves and others because without a spiritual identity to bring a sense of a Divine presence in their lives during their moments of crisis, they may see no reason to value life. Again, I am not suggesting that this is the only reason youth hurt themselves or others, but I am suggesting that the spiritual wasteland many youth live in takes a toll on their lives. It sometimes even takes their lives!

All children can be given a spiritual reservoir by parents, which can lead to a life-sustaining faith. Even if we adults have only the faith the size of a grain of mustard seed (a mere speck), we can help our children develop a relationship with God. When we are blessed with children, we must work at our faith and learn about the spiritual gifts our children need to grow a strong faith of their own. We shouldn't be frightened by this task. We are willing to work hard to save money for college. A life-sustaining spiritual identity is at least as important for our children's future. Remember, Justin Martyr's father did not teach his son all Justin would eventually teach others. He didn't try to give Justin all the answers; but obviously Justin's father encouraged the spiritual side of the young man's life. He must have encouraged Justin as a boy to wonder about important things, to consider his purpose here on earth. And that was enough. It was enough for Justin to develop a profound yearning, which led him to God.

I believe modern parents can help their children in the same way. Children must learn from their parents that they are valued not just as a person loved by a few family members and friends, but as a child loved by God. We parents can do this by first conveying to our children that there is more in our lives than human pleasures and pains. We may lead very average lives, but our lives will be great in our children's eyes if we point our lives to God. Our words need not be theologically sophisticated, but if we systematically encourage our children to seek God each day, they will grow toward that light.

Our children don't need to believe what we believe. They don't need us to give them all the answers to their questions. We should not try to indoctrinate them into one catechism. But we must consciously give them personal examples of our own faithful, if incomplete, spiritual journey toward God.

All the great theologians I have mentioned have insights for parents. St. Paul reminded us that it is through our personal relationship with the Son of God that we are transported beyond a vague notion of godliness to a very personal relationship with God in the form of the man from Nazareth. First

Philo, then Irenaeus from his uniquely Christian perspective, emphasized the importance of our inner spiritual connection to God. Finally, St. Augustine and Karl Barth taught us that in the gift of a child, we have been given a new chance to embark on a spiritual journey toward God. This begins with rediscovering our own yearnings for God.

All these teachings come together for parents when we read the plural reference to God in Genesis as creating a sacred triangular relationship between our child, us, and God. This "us" should be present at the creation (or adoption) of every child. This sacred relationship can be played out in a thousand small ways every day. Parents must understand that we can do nothing of lasting good for our children unless we first convey to them that they are children of God. Remember, Augustine reminded us that the child's capacity to have faith in God is only potential. If that potential is to be realized, it must begin with us. Children reach for God by standing on the shoulders of their parents.

Young children have a natural tendency to believe in the goodness of people. This is part of their spiritual nature. Although this quality can die from the neglect of adults or be perverted into a negative element if the wrong mentors take over our job, it is a powerful and positive force at the beginning of a child's life. Perhaps they come to us with this innate spiritual quality because they have been so recently in the presence of God. Martin Luther captured this idea in a Christmas sermon. He said, "For the higher people are in the favor of God, the more tender are they."

Parents who speak unapologetically about the importance of faith and about their belief in God's presence in their lives offer their children the first and most important spiritual gift. Martin Luther, in his famous sixteenth-century sermon on the nativity I mentioned above, reminded his congregation that when Mary and Joseph first looked upon the baby Jesus, Scripture says "they adored." What parents haven't looked at their child with similar feelings? We must also consider what the child is looking at. If, as our children grow, they see us looking not just at ourselves and not just at them, but they see us looking toward God, they will learn from this and look to God as well. Have you ever come upon a group of people looking up? We instinctively look up as well. Our children are watching how we live our lives, and if our lives are looking up toward God, they will look up as well.

In the chapters that follow, we will explore specifically some of the day-to-day things a parent can do to direct a child toward God. But for now, it is most important to establish this principle: Parents stand in the footsteps of the Almighty, we must be imitators of God, and it is our responsibility to help our children develop their capacity for faith in God. This capacity enables a child to develop a personal relationship with God. From this first principle comes everything important we need to know about being a parent.

Once I was lecturing on this subject to a church group, and a father interrupted me at about this point and asked, "When is it too late to start this? My daughter is eight."

The story of Justin proves that it is never too late to begin pointing a young person's life toward God. The burden, as well as the great joy of parenting, is that every day we have opportunities to direct our children beyond our imperfect example toward the perfect God. The principles behind our actions have a more profound impact on our children than anything we do. There is no need for us to fear making a mistake. We need only believe that God will take care of us and our children if we believe in God and try to walk with God.

One of the simplest and most profound ideas in the Bible is that God knows each of us and cares for us. God is parent-like in God's concern for us. God has high expectations for our personal behavior and a keen interest in our everyday life. In fact, we are assured in Scripture that God knows us so well that God has actually numbered the hairs on our head. This is a comfort and an assurance all children need as they leave us for a sometimes hostile world.

A young man once told me that Psalm 23 summed up how God was present in his life. As it does for many other people, this familiar psalm comforted him in his darkest moments. However, he surprised me when he said he could remember the exact day the psalm came alive for him. He had learned the words in church when he was very young, but his father had taught him their real meaning.

It was the first day of fishing season, and at the age of seven he was allowed to accompany his father, along with dozens of others, to the reservoir dam. The young man remembered being apprehensive about the excursion because, although he had fished with his father before, he never fished on opening day at the crowded dam.

In the past, he had stood with his mother and watched the scene as scores of fathers and sons lined the walk over the spillway of the dam. Standing shoulder to shoulder, they would put their lines in the water at the moment the official beginning of fishing season was announced. That worried the boy, because the boys and fathers often didn't stand together. From the vantage point of the shore, the men and boys on the walkway looked liked a great confusion of bodies, with the children separated from the fathers. The boy harbored the fear that with so many people, he would get lost. Furthermore, what would happen if he caught a fish? He would need help landing it. He wouldn't know what to do even if he did manage to get a fish to the walkway; he had never taken out a hook before. His father always did that. He was afraid of losing the fish and of being embarrassed if his father wasn't there to help.

He told me he actually wished he wouldn't catch a fish that day, to avoid his fears coming true. But, alas, he caught one of the first fish. Although he wasn't sure where his father was, he instinctively called out, "Daddy, I caught a . . ." Before he could say "fish," his father was at his side. ". . . [F]or thou art with me."

Obviously, the father wasn't very far away from the boy and, surely, he was very attentive to what the boy was doing. But, at the time, the boy didn't know that. He had only his father's assurance to rely upon, and that turned out to be enough. All he knew was that when the need arose, his father was at his side. The boy made the connection between that event, his faith in his father, and Psalm 23. It was a connection the boy carried with him into manhood.

Anonymity

What young people fear most are anonymity and insignificance. They want to fit in with their peers, but they want to be known and valued as individuals, as well. When they face terrifying moments that can lead to desperation, friends and family can offer only so much support. We might not agree that what the young person is facing is all that important; we might have lived through worse. However, we must recognize that the importance of any given situation in life can only be assigned by the person involved. No matter the situation, if we supply our children with even the most rudimentary foundation of faith, if we reassure them that we are made in God's image and because of that He will always care for them, then they can draw on that spiritual reservoir and develop their own life-sustaining companionship with God.

Naomi Rosenblatt wrote about this in her book *Wrestling with Angels*:[17]

Everything flows from the concept of God creating man and woman in His own image. If we feel deep within that we have been created in the image of God, then no matter where we are or what we are going through we never feel alone. We are never anonymous.

**Ten Things Parents Can Do
to Help Children Develop Healthy Spiritual Identities**

1. Take your children to church, and let them see you worship God.

2. Say prayers with your child before bed. It's a great time to reflect on the day. Let your child hear you ask God for forgiveness.

3. Pray over meals. This reminds everyone that all good things come from God. Prayers over meals should be confined to private events. Showy prayers in restaurants are like the theatrics of end-zone prayers—they cheapen an important moment.

4. Let your children hear you include "God talk" in meaningful family events. For example, include prayer as part of your decision-making process.

5. Tell young children stories from the Bible, don't just read them. Learn the stories and then tell them using your own words. A child's imagination is better than any illustrator's pen. Let them hear God's stories from you.

6. Remember always, the relationship with your child is triangular: you, your child, and God.

7. Encourage children to take their spiritual lives seriously. They can take it from there.

8. Engage in gratuitous service to others and let your child see you. Show your child that "Faith without works is dead."

9. Engage in study of Scripture and let your child see you doing it.

10. Remind your children that faith in God can build a spiritual reservoir they can draw on for strength the rest of their lives.

Chapter 2

Finding God

*O*nce children are in the world outside the home, many new influences begin to shape them. Often, whatever is new in their lives becomes preferred, and the family's values begin to be challenged with increasing frequency and energy. Parents should remember that the biblical God is a big God and God's message will win out over any transitory challenges. God is everywhere and always eager to become our child's companion. It is our responsibility to prepare our children to begin their own spiritual journey. In order to be prepared, our children must learn how to find God in their lives, in the world of school, and in activities outside the home. No one can find God for another person, but parents can help. The ability to find God in the world outside the home, as part of the preparation necessary for our child's own spiritual journey, is the second spiritual gift of a parent to a child.

C. S. Lewis believed that each of us must be brought into the "great hall" of Christianity before we can discover a true faith of our own. There are many ways into God's house. But, when it is the parent who leads the child, when it is the parent who introduces the child to the "house rules" of the Christian faith, a special bond is created between parent and child that transcends the worldly distractions. Once inside the great hall, the child can begin her own exploration of what Lewis called the "several rooms" of denominational affiliation from which one can choose.[1] Lewis called this introduction to the rudiments of biblical faith "mere Christianity," the Christian faith in its simplest form.

It is difficult, however, to find this hall on one's own. Parents must lead their children by the hand, for it is not until the child is inside the great hall that her own spiritual journey can begin. Developing a mature faith requires being able to recognize God in one's daily life as well as knowing where among the clutter and distractions of our busy world God is waiting for us.

A Patient God

The gospel stories and the lessons from the early church teach us that our God has chosen not to communicate with us in the same way God did with the first patriarchs of the Old Testament. The story of Moses is particularly instructive on this point. The personal encounter with God that Moses experienced on the holy mountain was dramatic and very unique. When Moses heard the voice of God coming from a burning bush, he was not expecting to talk with God. This story was not preserved just to impress us with the importance of Moses. Subtly tucked in the description of that first meeting is an important reference which, when properly understood, creates a powerful metaphor that can help every person's search for God. It is, most of all, a metaphor we can share with our children to help them prepare for their own spiritual journeys and encounters with God.

To understand what the story of Moses has to do with us, we must look carefully at some of the clues embedded in the story. First, when Moses sees the burning bush off in the distance, he stops to see what it could mean:

> Then Moses said, "I must turn aside and look at this great sight, and see why the bush is not burned up." *When the Lord saw that he had turned aside* to see, God called to him out of the bush, "Moses, Moses!" [my emphasis] (Exod. 3:3–4)

Notice that before God speaks, God waits for Moses to notice God's presence. This is an important characteristic of God: God chooses to patiently wait for us. Generations after this story, God also waited for the world to notice the divine presence in the form of the baby Jesus in a cradle in a barn in Bethlehem. Tell this story to your children: Just as God waited for the people lounging in the inn and for Moses to turn aside, God waits for us.

Another characteristic of the story of Moses that is important for any faith journey is that God is not found only in familiar circumstances. Moses saw the burning bush while in a foreign land. Despite the strangeness of the surroundings and the many things on Moses' mind (remember, he was a fugitive from Pharaoh), he took the time to explore the wonders around him—and that proved to be a great blessing not only to him, but to us all. This point is particularly important for parents to understand. This is not the biblical equivalent of "stop and smell the roses along the way"; rather, it is a reminder that God is always present in our lives, no matter where we are, if we will only look carefully around us.

Finally, the burning bush was not in the middle of Moses' path. He had to travel out of his way in order to explore its mysteries. God often chooses not to block our path. In fact, as we will see later, blocking one's path is more characteristic of the devil. God waits for us to recognize the divine presence in the events of our lives. This characteristic of God shows us that the spiritual dimension of our lives cannot be placed in a segmented compartment. Our spiritual life *is* our secular life. We need not take to the monastery or even to a holy mountain to find God. God is waiting for us in our workplace, in our homes, in our schools, and along the pathways of our lives. Scripture assures us that God is there, perhaps in unusual forms, always patiently waiting for us to see things in a new way, sometimes reminding us what is important. To my surprise, but I suspect not to hers, my mother had to remind me about this. She had taught this lesson to me as a young boy, but, ironically, she had to remind me of it again, just when I thought I was getting closer to God. As with Moses, her lesson came to me in what was for me a "new land," one as distracting for me as perhaps Sinai was for Moses. She had to teach me again that you can never tell where God will find you. God could even be, as the saying goes, looking at us through the eyes of the beggar.

Through the Eyes of the Beggar

During my first year in seminary, I made infrequent visits home to see my widowed mother. I didn't even call much. Life was too busy. However, for Mother's Day of that year, perhaps motivated by guilt, I sent my mother a bus ticket from her northeastern Pennsylvania home to New York City. My modest gesture (although grand for my financial circumstances at the time) was part of a plan for us to meet, go to a Broadway matinee, drive the hour back to Princeton (where I attended theological seminary), and stay at my apartment for the evening. The following day I intended to show her the seminary and introduce her to my new friends.

I could tell from her voice on the phone that she was thrilled when she received the ticket. Although she had spent most of her life only a few hours from New York City, she hadn't traveled much and had rarely visited "the city." I also knew she missed me. Because I had gone to college in my hometown, we remained close during my college years. During that time, my father had died and much of my mother's social life in the years following his death had revolved around an enthusiastic group of football players' parents who traveled together to each of my college games. After four years of trips and games, all that was gone from her daily life, including me.

I was also looking forward to seeing her. Her visit would give me a chance to show off my new life. I was enjoying seminary; it was an intellectually and spiritually stimulating experience. But my "field work" placement was truly eye-opening for me. I worked on the weekends as a helper at a drug rehabilitation center in the Greenwich Village section of Manhattan. At the end of a week of classes, all seminarians were expected to spend the weekend in some field-work experience. My time in this field-work assignment had made me confident that I could maneuver around the city like an experienced New Yorker. I had acquired the protective shell that I thought city life required of its inhabitants.

Mother arrived in New York on a beautiful May afternoon. I showed her the drug treatment center, and she marveled that such a place and such desperate young people existed. After that we were off; first lunch, then the play. The warm sunshine combined with the fun of being together made for a wonderful day. We talked non-stop. Mother asked lots of questions and wanted to know about the people whom I had met and what life was like for me. I could tell with each story my mom was pleased and proud of me.

Then something happened that changed the whole experience. As we made our way to the parking garage to get my Volkswagen, we passed a street person sprawled out into the center of the sidewalk. I gently guided my mother around him and hardly interrupted my commentary. She, however, hung back. I guessed that she had never before seen a homeless person. Although she had grown up poor, and our family was of very modest means, our working-class neighborhood was clean, safe, and supportive. When someone lost a job, the neighbors helped out until another was found. No one took to the streets in my hometown, at least not in 1971.

My mother continued to resist my pressing on. "What's wrong with him?" she asked, looking back.

"He's OK. He's just a street person, homeless. They are everywhere in the city," I assured her, not really knowing much about the plight of the homeless. "That's all an act to get tourists to give them money," I embellished.

My mother fell silent as we walked, and I knew something was wrong. She seemed less interested in my stories of life in bucolic Princeton. Finally she said, "I think I want to go back home tonight."

Her comment rocked me. "Why? What's wrong? I thought you wanted to see the seminary."

"You should have helped that man."

"What man?"

"The street person," she said emphatically, annoyed.

In my most practiced and ivy-covered rhetoric, I explained to her that these people were not for real, they were panhandlers, actors playing on our sympathies. Only out-of-towners ever paid any attention to them. But she remained silent.

"I thought you wanted to see the seminary," I pressed, with a touch of pout that was carefully measured to move my mother in my direction. But she replied with her usual brand of wisdom, "If that's what they are teaching there, I don't want to see it."

As I grew up, my mother had taught me the precepts of the Christian faith. She was the person who had taken me by the hand into the great hall of Christianity. Her faith was not complicated nor doctrinally based. It was beautifully summed up, however, in the words of her favorite hymn, "who serves the Father as a son is truly kin to me."[2] Although I was an adult and she was no theologian, she had to teach her seminarian son yet again. In the biblical faith I received from her, I knew to serve the Lord was to serve those in need, but despite the fact that I was on my way to becoming a minister, I had forgotten where to look for God in my everyday life. When Jesus said, "For you always have the poor with you . . ." (Matt. 26:11), he was not making a prediction; he was assuring us that there will always be ample ways of serving him.

You can't predict where God will be. Remember on that first Easter when Mary stood weeping at the empty tomb? At a sound, she turns but mistakes Jesus for a gardener:

> Jesus said to her, "Woman, why are you weeping? Whom are you looking for?" Supposing him to be the gardener, she said to him, "Sir, if you have carried him away, tell me where you have laid him, and I will take him away." Jesus said to her, "Mary!" She turned and said to him in Hebrew, "Rabbouni!" (which means Teacher). (John 20:15–16)

He goes on to surprise his disciples. After the resurrection, Jesus confronts them as they flee Jerusalem in fear and confusion after his death:

> Now on that same day two of them were going to a village called Emmaus, about seven miles from Jerusalem, and talking with each other about all these things that had happened. While they were talking and discussing, Jesus himself came near and went with them, but their eyes were kept from recognizing him.

> When he was at the table with them, he took bread, blessed and broke it, and gave it to them. Then their eyes were opened, and they recognized him; and he vanished from their sight. (Luke 24:13–16, 30–31)

Finding God is all about opening our eyes. The eyes of the Levites and priests were closed as they passed the robbed and beaten man, but it was the Samaritan who was moved to pity and action. Did the Samaritan recognize something in the eyes of that beaten man? It was the hated Samaritan who stopped to help, but because Jesus told us of his kindness, his is the action held up to us as a model for Christian action. In my case, I was preparing to become a "priest" in the church, but my eyes were closed; I was ready to walk to the other side. I had forgotten the lesson of the Good Samaritan. So, my mother had to teach it to me again. One is called to parenthood for life.

Martin Luther challenged his congregation during a Christmas sermon nearly four hundred years ago to open their eyes. Luther scolded:

> There are many of you in this congregation who think to yourselves: "If only I had been there! How quick I would have been to help the Baby! I would have washed his linen. How happy I would have been to go with the shepherds to see the Lord lying in the manger!" Yes, you would! You say that because you know how great Christ is, but if you had been there at that time you would have done no better than the people of Bethlehem. Childish and silly thoughts are these! Why don't you do it now? You have Christ in your neighbor. You ought to serve him, for what you do to your neighbor in need you do the Lord Christ himself.[3]

On a Mother's Day in New York, I was reminded by my mother, through her disappointment, that in all my excitement about seminary and my new life, I shouldn't forget the most fundamental lessons of our faith.

> Truly I tell you, just as you did it to one of the least of these who are members of my family, you did it to me. (Matt. 25:40)

Jesus' reference to helping family brings us to another important clue about helping our children find God in their lives. The Greek word for *family* used in this verse does not refer to what we might call the nuclear family but, rather, the one large family of humankind. Thus, we can tell our children that God calls us into human relationships as a way of revealing God's self to us.

Of Mice and Gorillas

> For where two or three are gathered in my name, I am there among them. (Matt. 18:20)

God's presence in worship is a powerful concept for our children to grasp. It is, however, one of the many experiences lost on some of today's youth.

Few young people attend a solemn assembly of any kind. Concerts and games are as close as many youth come to being in a large crowd of their peers. Although I have spent most of my life in private schools with both required religion courses and chapel services, few of my students have identified themselves as churchgoers. Obviously, their families were choosing the schools for reasons other than to support the religious inclinations of the family. In my informal polls over the years, no more than one-third of my students in any given year said they attended church regularly with their parents. Usually the number was much lower. Today, children are rarely asked to sit quietly in a large room filled with people and think about something other than themselves. The idea of the spirit of God transforming a gathering into a sacred assembly is foreign to many people. If you have recently attended a movie, you know the behavior of people, especially younger people, is often appalling. Today, many people have difficulty sitting quietly even when they are being entertained.

How do we teach ill-disciplined young people the idea of sacred space? The first step is making sure that after worship children understand what was said in church. For example, in a conversation with his son after church, a father was surprised that his son thought the minister had blessed the congregation, "In the name of the Father, and the Son, and the Whole East Coast!"

I spoke with a Sunday school teacher who wasn't sure she was making progress with her first grade class. In a discussion about God, one child had asked God's name. She explained that we just call God, "God," preferring not to get into the Hebrew derivative "Yahweh" with her young class. But one of the 6-year-olds told the class that he knew God's name. "Oh really?" the teacher stumbled. "What do you think God's name is?" she asked. "Howard," came the reply. "Howard? Why do you think that is God's name?" the teacher asked. "We pray to him every night. Our Father who art in heaven," began the child, "Howard be thy name!"

Teaching young people about sacred space requires good adult examples. Sadly, young people sometimes have more reverence for sacred space than do adults. At one of the boarding schools where I served as chaplain, we had morning chapel services for about twenty minutes twice each week. There was a tacit acceptance of the week-day service among the students. The students were required to attend, but only about 20 percent of the faculty did. At the school I had several responsibilities: In addition to serving as chaplain, I taught, coached football, and lived in a dormitory. I had a very close relationship with the students. But, my ministry had the support of only a small group of the faculty. Most of them, I felt, resented the school's having a chaplain. They preferred that the daily routine of the school not be interrupted by chapel services. When I suggested a service for the entire school community on Sundays, I received no support from the faculty. Despite the fact that the school's great colonial chapel dominated the campus, religion had been crowded into an inconspicuous corner of school life.

One morning, just after the first hymn of the chapel service, a student in a gorilla suit came bounding down the center aisle. The students were momentarily stunned, then broke into riotous laughter. The ape stopped in front of the pulpit, scratched himself in mock curiosity, and then quickly exited by a side door. I had no idea what to do. I stood at the pulpit and waited for the laughter to stop, and then proceeded with my brief morning meditation. But, I was devastated. The sacred place I had been working hard to create for the students, the one place that was supposed to be about God and not us, had been violated. I was angry. What annoyed me most was the faculty reaction afterward. Most enjoyed the schoolboy prank and saw nothing venial, but others saw it as the tip of a massive protest building within the student body against required chapel. My friends on the faculty were silenced by this interpretation, and the headmaster seemed paralyzed.

Throughout the day I sulked. In my classes, my students wanted to know what I thought of the prank. I told them that I thought it was funny but an inappropriate prank because gathering for worship changes a place from our place to God's house. I had great discussions with my students about the prank. The event had turned into a wonderful teaching moment. My students wanted to know more about the idea of sacred space, so we talked about God commanding Moses to take off his shoes before the burning bush, the first sacred space of Yahweh. The idea of changing a space because of its use seemed to strike a chord with them. I wanted them to understand that the events of the day were troubling to me not because a school assembly was interrupted, but because the worship of God was mocked.

Later that evening, a student knocked on my dormitory apartment door. When I opened the door, a downcast boy stood there. "I did it," was all he said. "You!" I roared, releasing some of the anger I had built up all day. "You!!!" We spoke only briefly because I felt myself losing my temper and didn't want the boy to receive the full brunt of what was building inside of me. I was upset that this boy was involved. He was a boy I had taught and counseled during a difficult time in his life. I felt I had a good relationship with him, but now I was overwhelmed with a sense of betrayal. Despite my anger, the boy managed to get out a few sentences he had rehearsed. He said, "I only meant it as a joke. I didn't mean it as disrespect. I like chapel. We all do. I am sorry."

I learned afterward that several students had prevailed upon him to come forward. These students sensed that a movement was afoot among the faculty to make the incident have more meaning than it was intended to have. The gorilla costume was a joke, not a student protest. When word spread as to why I was upset, it struck a chord. They, too, wanted sacred time and place in their school life.

Once they are pointed in the right direction, young people seem to sense the importance of special places and of sacred time. The scene from the movie *The Dead Poet's Society*, when the students gather in the cave, beautifully depicts adolescent recognition of sacred space and spiritual moments. As the movie shows, unless these sacred spaces and spiritual moments are shaped by something as profound as Christianity, they remain mere cults.

It was years later, while I was serving as chaplain in another school, that another student prank taught me that when we adults care enough to teach children about the importance of worship, they get it. This school had a required Sunday evening chapel service. All the school gathered in the chapel after dinner to begin our new week of boarding school life together in worship. I learned at the previous school to always explain why worship is important—how invoking God's presence in one's life should not be trivialized into audacious displays of religion like kneeling in prayer after catching a touchdown pass, but rather celebrated in quiet moments together in worship. I learned that creating ownership of the worship service by including students in the service as readers, as speakers, and through musical performance personalizes the worship experience for them and adds an important dimension.

One night, as I stood to begin my sermon, I noticed a flash of white light on the floor. When I tried to focus on it, it was gone. Then there was another, and then it was gone too. After the second flash, I realized that I wasn't seeing light but something crawling on the floor of the chapel. The entire student body and faculty were present, and the chapel was full. I hesitated before beginning to speak. Three hundred and fifty students and faculty looked at me, wondering why I wasn't preaching. Then there was another flash. It was a white mouse! Tittering began among the students. Now there were dozens of little critters dashing along the red carpet, in and out of pews. I stood frozen at the pulpit. Seminary doesn't prepare you for this.

In a moment, after some shuffling, the mice were gone. I could see some of the older students elbowing others to be quiet. One faculty member stood up and moved next to a group of students who seemed to be particularly enjoying the event. They quieted down. The chapel fell silent. That night I preached my sermon to an unusually attentive student body.

Afterward, I learned that a group of students had decided that the white mice in the science building would make hilarious visitors to chapel. The little white flashes of light I saw were tucked in their pockets and were released just as I was making my way to the pulpit. One of the most respected teachers at the school, who was sitting with his wife, quickly figured out what was happening and leaned down and snatched one of the little critters from the floor. The students around him, out of respect, did the same. In the next few moments, without any words being spoken, the mice were gone. Apparently the students listened to my sermon that night while little creatures squirmed in their pockets. This teacher's actions were more about one man's acknowledgment of sacred space than about me, God, or even mice.

That teacher taught me a great deal about how young people come to value sacred space. He commanded the respect of the students in the classroom and on the field and used that respect to teach another lesson. He didn't have to talk; his actions were clear enough. Young people simply have to be shown what to do. When they see respect being given, they will give it as well.

Once, a senior faculty member grabbed me just before the closing baccalaureate service the day before graduation. One of the duties of the older man was to be the head usher for the service. The guest speaker was ready, and the headmaster and faculty were ready to process into the chapel. However, there was a problem. A boy who had been dismissed from school months earlier had shown up for the ceremony. I was told he was either drunk or on drugs. He had chosen to sit conspicuously in the middle of the section reserved for faculty. He lounged defiantly with both arms stretched out over the back of the pew; he sat there with a hat on.

The senior master was in a panic. Nobody seemed to know what to do and, although I had no formal part in this ceremony, he wondered what I planned to do about this problem.

I was very conscious that the audience grew quieter as I walked to the reserved section at the front of the chapel. I had no idea what I was going to say to this potentially intoxicated and agitated young man. He sensed my movement toward him and he turned to me. "So, they sent you to get me out of here," he said. "No," I said, "I just thought you should take your hat off in chapel," I responded. I could tell the young man was temporarily disarmed by my response. "Oh, sorry," he said, and he took off his hat. I said, "By the way, this section is reserved for the faculty, but I'll get you a good seat in the right place if you like." He started to laugh, "Oh, I just thought no one wanted to sit with me." We both laughed, and he moved. Sacred places can have a powerful and sobering effect on everyone.

"He intended to pass them by"

God can be revealed through human relationships, the events of our lives as well as through sacred places. Although God has infinite patience and waits for us to come to God's house, we should not think that God is passive. Our children should know that God *actively* waits, both in the events that consume our lives as well as in the events that have yet to unfold in our lives. The Bible is rich with imagery of a God who goes ahead of us to await our arrival. There are times when we can follow these footsteps, especially when we don't know exactly where we should be going. One story from Mark's gospel is particularly instructive on this point:

> When he saw that they were straining at the oars against an adverse wind, he came towards them early in the morning, walking on the sea. He intended to pass them by. But when they saw him walking on the sea, they thought it was a ghost and cried out; for they all saw him and were terrified. But immediately he spoke to them and said, "Take heart, it is I; do not be afraid." Then he got into the boat with them and the wind ceased. And they were utterly astounded. (Mark 6:48–52)

The story of Jesus walking on water occurs in three Gospels: Matthew, Mark, and John; however, in each account, there are differences. The story as recorded in Mark is worth a special look from us, for like the story of Moses and the burning bush, an additional detail in Mark's account of this story is worth parents' special consideration. Especially notice verse 48b: "He intended to pass them by." In Mark's account, Jesus is not walking on the water toward the boat, as he is in the other Gospel accounts; rather, in Mark, Jesus is intending to pass the disciples' boat. Where is he going? Why would he not be coming to the aid of his struggling disciples as they pull on the oars against the wind?

Verse 48b is not an oddity of translation or an idea unique to Mark. This image comes from the Hebrew Scripture, and Mark used it in his descriptions elsewhere. For example, early in Jesus' ministry, when the disciples were first trying to piece together the meaning of Jesus' teachings, Jesus is described as physically ahead of them, waiting for them to catch up, waiting for them to catch on.

> They were on the road, going up to Jerusalem, and Jesus was walking ahead of them; they were amazed, and those who followed were afraid. (Mark 10:32)

The Old Testament references that Mark draws upon include this passage from Exodus where God speaks to Moses:

> I am going to send an angel in front of you, to guard you on the way and to bring you to the place that I have prepared. (Exod. 23:20)

We have in these words a powerful metaphor for helping our children gain the spiritual sight needed to find God. We can tell them that God is omnipresent, present in those who need our help and present in our future. Jesus reassures us of this: "And if I go and prepare a place for you, I will come again and will take you to myself, so that where I am, there you may be also" (John 14:3). For this reason, we need not be afraid of the future or of any new and uncertain events in our lives. We can tell our children that they can move ahead with confidence into their futures, confident that God is a trustworthy God awaiting their arrival: a God who has already prepared a place for them.

There is a story I have heard in many different forms. I don't know where it comes from, but it is a story every child should hear. It is about a man who has a dream, and in it he sees the events of his life. Between the events, good and bad, is a second image of two sets of footprints in the sand of a beach. The man senses that one set was his and the other footprints were God's. But there was something very troubling about this image. For he noticed that during the darkest moments of his life—the death of his parents, a broken heart in school, when he was cut from the baseball team as a young boy, or when he lost his job—there was only one set of footsteps in the sand. The man asked God why, during his life's darkest moments, had God not been with him? God laughed and said, "My precious son, when you were most alone, afraid and downcast, I carried you."

Moratorium

Moving from childbearing through child rearing is a path with many twists and turns. One twist that often unnerves parents is the rather predictable resistance of children who do not want to attend church. This battle is usually fought during the middle and high school years. Many parents worry that their child's resistance to church attendance constitutes a rejection of the Church, religion, and faith in general. To reassure those in the throes of this battle with their children, or those who will someday face it, I offer a slightly different way of looking at the problem.

In both Luke and Matthew,[4] unnamed disciples beg for postponement of the time they must begin to follow Jesus. When discussing these scenes with my students, it is common for them to identify closely with the would-be disciples. Often they say of those reluctant disciples, "Maybe they just weren't ready."

Sometimes, young people just aren't ready for God. Erik Erikson, a psycho-social theorist, observed this in the adolescents with whom he worked. Sometimes, adolescents react to the storms within themselves by prematurely committing to something before they are ready. Erikson called this "role confusion."[5] This characteristic propelled Martin Luther toward a premature decision to become an Augustinian monk. It is not uncommon for adolescents to be willing to commit to a cause without sufficient reflection. However, many other teenagers have a different reaction. They are paralyzed by the emotional and hormonal storms within, and thus are unable to make any commitments at all. At times, young people are so completely self-absorbed that it is not over-identification that evolves but a kind of spiritual inertia.

We parents need not become anxious about this spiritual stagnation. Remember, our God is a patient God, and we must be patient parents. God understands all human conditions, even the need for the occasional moratorium, a temporary time-out before resuming one's spiritual journey.

The philosopher Simone Weil reflected on her own need for a moratorium during her adolescence:

> As soon as I reached adolescence, I saw the problem of God as a problem the data of which could not be obtained here below, and I decided that the only way of being sure not to reach the wrong solution, which seemed to me the greatest possible evil, was to leave it alone. So I left it alone. I neither affirmed nor denied anything.[6]

෴෴෴

Years ago, while working as a boarding school chaplain, I responded to the academic dean's request for a new religion course elective. Over the summer, I developed a course on the religious history of the American people. However, as the next term drew closer, I became apprehensive that the material I had chosen was too challenging for high school students. I was pleased to find the name of one of the brightest girls in the school on the class roster. I felt sure that with the help of a student of her caliber in class discussions, the course would be a success. She would understand the material and be the student to whom I could turn in class to help other students grasp the point. However, at the start of the school year, my optimism faded quickly.

To my chagrin, my prized student rarely spoke in class. My best attempts to draw her into the conversations didn't work. On top of this disappointment, I knew the course wasn't going well for the rest of the class. Most students found the material too dense, the issues remote, and my explanations convoluted. My frustration mounted with the students' increasing unhappiness. I grew resentful that my best student sat silently as my little boat was being blown toward the academic shoals.

One day, in an unfortunate display of pedagogical bad form, I asked my prize student to stay behind after class. I asked her what she thought of the course, the material, the assignments, and the structure of the discussions. I could tell she was unnerved by the interview. However, she allowed that she found the course "fine." That did it. Fine! I was losing the big game, and my star player was choosing to stay in the stands!

In a thinly veiled sarcastic tone, I said that I was surprised she thought the class was "fine," because she rarely spoke. I told her I was disappointed that she was not participating more in the discussions. I asked her why she had taken the class if she wasn't going to contribute. The uncommon maturity that my fellow faculty members had assured me she possessed came out in her response. She told me she only enrolled in the class because of her roommate, who had been my student in another class the year earlier. During night-long conversations, her roommate had told her of the questions I was raising in class and how they had caused her to think about her own faith in a new way.

Then my student said something that reminded me of Erikson's comment about the occasional need for moratorium in a young person's life. She said, "I took your course because I wanted to hear you talk about God." She told me that she had been reared in a family without religion; her parents never talked about faith, and she did not know whether her parents believed anything at all. She had questions, however. She wasn't sure she wanted to get involved in any kind of spiritual journey. She wasn't sure if she even wanted to have a spiritual life. She knew she needed time and space to think about these things, and my class gave her both the distance from and the closeness to the topic she needed. This was her moratorium. She wasn't sure she was ever going to be a participant in the class discussions; however, the course was stimulating her thinking, and she was grateful for the opportunity the class offered her.

All good teachers come to understand the need of young people to occasionally prefer to keep an intellectual distance from powerful topics. In *Coming Apart: A Memoir of the Harvard Wars of 1969,* Roger Rosenblatt makes an interesting observation that teachers and parents should heed. He writes:

> What the brighter students honor in their favorite teachers is the quality of worry. They like to see teachers worry about the material, and they like to overhear them worry. That, I think, is what the best teaching is—being overheard as one worries aloud about a subject.[7]

Some adults misinterpret children's silence or cool boredom as disinterest. Sometimes, students are not disinterested, but they simply prefer to passively absorb. Those of us who have an opportunity to stimulate a child's spiritual thinking ought not to shrink from the task. They want us to "worry" about spiritual issues in front of them. Sometimes the very process of observing adult spiritual "worry" can help move the young person into a more active struggle with faith issues.

Parents and teachers of adolescents must be ready to give the safe distance needed for young people to think about something as powerful as the biblical God. When middle school students want to stop going to church, I usually tell parents, "Let them stay home." This, of course, does not suggest that church programs especially designed for young people are not worthwhile. In fact, I would argue strongly that we need more cross-generational church programs that are better designed to meet the unique needs of young people and their families. Yet, we must also be prepared to be patient. Remember, the proverb is specific: "Train children in the right way, and when old, they will not stray" (Prov. 22:6). Notice, the proverb is silent on the time between when a person is young and when a person is old. We do not need to fret about our young people dropping behind for a while, distracted by what seems more important to them at the time. They can catch up later.

If parents have brought their children into the great hall of Christianity when their children are between the ages of three and thirteen, it is safe to give them the distance they need thereafter. It has been my experience that if the seed of faith was properly planted and nurtured during those very early years, we can have confidence that it will sprout and eventually blossom in God's good time. However, a late planting is better than having nothing at all to harvest.

Ten Things a Parent Can Do
to Help a Child Find God

C.S. Lewis argues that a parent's responsibility is to bring a child into the great hall of Christianity. How can we do this?

1. Take a child from ages three through twelve to church. The child will learn two things:
    - The rudiments of faith—mere Christianity
    - The idea of sacred space

    These ideas cannot be learned through words; they can only be imparted through experience.

2. Assure your children that God is ahead of them, patiently waiting for them. If they seek God, God will find them.

3. Remind children that God can often be found in the eyes of the needy.

4. Show your child that you take your faith seriously by discussing the worship service on the way home. A few thoughtful words about the sermon, prayer, or music can convey reverence. Discuss how a portion of the service touched you.

5. Don't be afraid to give your children a break from God. If they met God as a child, they will return to their divine parent.

6. Tell children that God hides from us because it is only when we look for God are we ready to know God.

7. Lower your voice in church or better still, be quiet. It is the easiest way to teach the idea of sacred space.

8. Put your child in a school that requires community service and assemblies that call the student beyond him or herself to higher ideas. School chapel services are ideal, but sadly are available only in some private schools.

9. Let your child hear you "worry" about spiritual issues. Talk to your child about the spiritual dimension of everyday issues.

10. Remember you don't have to be a perfect spiritual parent, but you must fulfill your responsibility to your children by taking them into the great hall of Christianity.

Chapter 3

A Transcendent Perspective

Elie Wiesel, Nobel Laureate and Holocaust survivor, asks a haunting question: How could the Nazi guards who each night went home to their wives and children, listened to Wagner, read Goethe, and kissed their children good night, go to "work" the next day and lead innocent Jewish women and children to their deaths? Put another way, why don't education, culture, and the commonwealth of ideas lead to righteousness and human kindness? Wiesel knows that brutality, senseless violence, and self-destructive behavior are spiritual issues, not educational or political problems. All the education in the world, all the culture, the ballet, and the greatest works of art, can't change the human heart. The Nazis, the slave owners, and many other cruel oppressors in history were, in many cases, cultured people. But, to use a biblical phrase, their hearts were "hardened."

These kinds of observations are depressing. Will our age, with all the possibilities the age of information holds, turn out to be no different than the other failed social experiments of the past? Are we Americans, like the Romans, enjoying prosperity while our moral fiber rots?

Vaclav Havel, playwright and the first democratically elected president of the Czech Republic, also sees the political and social problems of our day as essentially due to a spiritual void in our modern world. He writes:

> The present crisis of authority is only one of a thousand consequences of the general crisis of spirituality in the world at present. Humankind, having lost its respect for a higher authority, has inevitably lost respect for earthly authority as well. Consequently, people also lose respect for their fellow humans and eventually even for themselves. This loss of transcendent perspective, to which everything on this Earth relates, inevitably leads to a collapse of earthly value systems as well. Humanity has lost what I

once privately described as the absolute horizon; and as a result, every-thing in life has become relative.[1]

A transcendent perspective of which Havel writes changes the way we look at things; it literally means to be able to look beyond what is in front of us. This is a godly perspective, a view of life that allows us to see things God's way. The Beatitudes are the perfect expression of God's way of seeing things. Only God could see the meek as inheriting the earth or happiness in mourning the death of a loved one. God's transcendent perspective helps us see beyond the events of our daily lives to the true meaning of life.

Those who call for the moral education of our children based on civic rather than godly values are fooling themselves. At the center of the prob-lem in our culture is what the modern Spanish philosopher Jose Ortega y Gassett describes as a lack of *creencias*, those "embedded certitudes and core convictions so taken for granted as not to be called into question."[2] The commentaries of both Havel and Gassett are like the observation of the writer of Judges: "In those days there was no king in Israel; all the people did what was right in their own eyes" (Judg. 21:25). Just like the sinful peo-ple of the past, we twenty-first-century Americans prefer to do our own thing, free from God. But, it seems that freedom only leads us to selfish-ness, and selfishness to brutality. The myth that there are common values flies in the face of the presumption in our society that everyone's opinion is of equal merit. However, when everything is of equal value, nothing is precious. If the Bible has one simple message for us all, it is that when we stand for nothing, we fall for everything.

Finding what is really important in life, what is reliable and certain, is hard work. It is also something that no one can do for us. There have always been those who have been willing to tell others what to think and believe. Cult leaders are certain about everything. Sometimes all religions, all churches, and any kind of faith are thrown into the same basket with cults. After all, don't all religions pretend to know all the answers?

These are the questions we have to help our children resolve. It doesn't mean we must have all the answers ourselves, but we must know where to point our children to find their own faith in God. For former generations, the link between the common events of daily life and the ultimate purpose of existence came through faith in God as expressed through organized reli-gion. In fact, the meaning, the root, of the word *religion* comes from the Latin word *religio* and that from *ligâre*, "to bind." At its best, faith in God expressed through religion simultaneously calls us to be bound to God and to our fellow human beings. Scripture promises us that when we have the gift of faith, we can discover for ourselves that "absolute horizon" of which Havel writes. A horizon doesn't give us all the answers, it simply orients us toward the light. It allows us to put our present circumstances in the proper perspective and to see beyond the immediate context of our lives to that which is of lasting value.

෧෧෧෧෧

Achieving a transcendent perspective changes the way we act. Once we see things God's way, we can never sit idle again. The connection between a godly perspective and right behavior is nowhere more beautifully preserved than in the story of Abraham. In this story from Genesis, one verse captures all the possibilities faith in God holds for us. The following was said of Abraham:

> "And he believed the LORD; and the LORD reckoned it to him as right-eousness." (Gen. 15:6)

This verse is so important that it is repeated by New Testament writers. It is held up to us by Paul and James[3] in their letters. The verse simply means that Abraham's faith in God changed him so much that everything he tried to do turned out to be good. Even when Abraham was uncertain, even when he was doing bad things, his faith in God was so powerful that good resulted from his actions. What an amazing God! The power in the transcendent perspective of God transformed Abraham's actions.

However, there are problems with the Abraham story. After all, isn't Abraham the biblical character who pretended his wife was his sister and allowed her to be sold into the Pharaoh's harem? Isn't this the man who impregnated his servant girl, and then cast her and her young child out into the wilderness? Isn't this the man who bound his child and prepared to sacrifice him like an animal?

Yes, this is our model of faith, a model of human imperfection held up to us as a model of faith. Why would God choose such a man? Because in Abraham's story, is our story. Let us look at him in his darkest moment to see the light God shone into his life.

Abraham's Mind

Our love for our children makes us vulnerable. When God punished King David in the Bible for his great sin of arranging the death of the warrior Uriah,

God chose the only punishment that would truly inflict pain into David's life. For putting Uriah at the front of the battle, and then ordering his troops withdrawn, David was responsible for Uriah's death—a murder arranged so that David could cover his adultery with Bathsheba, Uriah's wife.

David's punishment was through his children. David was a brave man. He could have withstood any punishment God would visit on him. But, to watch his children suffer eventually broke him. David watched as one of his own sons raped his only daughter and as another son killed that brother and then led a revolt against David's rule. Finally, he endured watching his best friend kill the son who had led the revolt. God spared David from the death he deserved for his crimes only to have him die a thousand times as his family destroyed itself.

David never recovered from the destruction of his family. Most parents never fully recover from the death of a child. I have a friend who has five siblings. One of her brothers died from an infection and the lack of antibiotics during World War II. My friend recalls a curious thing about her mother. Until her death, the mother kept only one picture on her bureau: the picture of the son who died. Of all the many happy events in that woman's life, it was that picture she chose to look at each day. No trauma that can befall an adult is more devastating than the death of a child. To die before your children, the saying goes, is to live a happy life. Therefore, hurting your child, not in rage, but with cold-blooded predetermination, conjures up a picture of an unspeakable monster. Yet, we are asked to consider Abraham—a man who appears to have considered just such an act— the father of our faith. It is this very act, the murder of his own dear child, that the great patriarch Abraham planned as he traveled toward Mt. Moriah, the place of sacrifice. What could he have been thinking?

Long before the story of the "binding of Isaac," God had promised Abraham that he would father a great nation. However, the elderly Abraham and his equally ancient wife, Sarah, had no children. Then, very late in life, a son was born to them. It was a miracle, a gift from God for which both Abraham and Sarah had prayed. What a joy Isaac must have been to this old man who had risked so much to follow his God. Here was a son, the link to all those future generations Abraham believed would come from him, should he only have the courage to faithfully follow this unnamed God. The birth of the boy was vindication. Abraham had followed God, and God's promises were finally beginning to come true.

Then a stunning demand came from God, stranger than all the commands before, a cruel command: Sacrifice the boy. John Calvin, the great sixteenth-century Protestant reformer and chief architect of early Protestant theology, wrote about Abraham's state of mind: "His mind . . . must of necessity have been severely crushed, and violently agitated, when the *command* and the *promise* of God were conflicting within him."[4] When my students come to this story in our reading of the Bible, they usually are incredulous. Frankly, it is difficult to get young people to become seriously engaged in the story. They find it bizarre. They see Abraham as a fanatic and his God as a cruel and heartless deity. Most parents just feel a little sick when we read Scripture's dispassionate account of God's command:

> Take your son, your only son Isaac, whom you love, and go to the land of Moriah, and offer him there as a burnt offering on one of the mountains that I shall show you. So Abraham rose early in the morning, saddled his donkey, and took two of his young men with him, and his son Isaac; he cut the wood for the burnt offering, and set out and went to the place in the distance that God had shown him. (Gen. 22:2–3)

My students can't get over the fact that God wanted a human sacrifice! They also get confused about Abraham's behavior. Why didn't he argue with God about the command to sacrifice Isaac as he did a few chapters earlier in defense of the people of Sodom and Gomorrah? The account in Genesis doesn't even say that Abraham asked God why God wanted Isaac sacrificed. The narrator simply writes, "so." My students are always skeptical that God could tell a man out of the blue to kill his son as a religious act and that all the narrator could offer as a link to the rest of the story is "so," as if what was to follow was a logical next step. Unsatisfied with God's command, my students are equally troubled by Abraham's silent acquiescence. In the years following the infamous Jonestown, Guyana, deathpact massacre,[5] my students drew parallels between that horrible event and the story of Abraham. To my students, the biblical Abraham was like a modern-day Jim Jones. They were all senseless religious fanatics.

I plead with my students to give Abraham a chance. I ask them to look at the whole story. I ask them to try to figure out why Abraham would have had faith in a God who had commanded such an incomprehensible act. I build my case by asking them to look at how Abraham came to the "Promised Land" in the first place. This passage is known as the "call" of Abraham:

> . . . . "Go from your country and your kindred and your father's house to the land that I will show you. I will make of you a great nation, and I will bless you, and make your name great, so that you will be a blessing." (Gen. 12:1–2)

Exactly how this call came to Abraham is not described in any detail and, thus, we can suppose the writer didn't think the mode of the message was important. Curiously, Abraham uprooted his family based on this message from God and moved them hundreds of miles away to a strange and hostile land. His response, at this point, was as unquestioning as it was later when he responded to God's command to sacrifice his son, Isaac, on Mt. Moriah.

Abraham, however, didn't always take God's commands with such willing acceptance. When God told Abraham of the plan to destroy the wretched towns of Sodom and Gomorrah because of their great sin, Abraham argued with God; in fact, he seemed to talk God out of the plan. Notice the contrast in how Abraham spoke to God in this instance:

> "Will you indeed sweep away the righteous with the wicked? Suppose there are fifty righteous within the city; will you then sweep away the place and not forgive it for the fifty righteous who are in it? Far be it from you to do such a thing, to slay the righteous with the wicked, so that the righteous fare as the wicked! Far be that from you! Shall not the Judge of all the earth do what is just?" And the LORD said, "If I find at Sodom fifty righteous in the city, I will forgive the whole place for their sake." (Gen. 18:23–26)

Abraham continued his negotiation until God agreed to reduce the number of righteous men needed to save the towns to a mere ten.

The relationship between Abraham and God was complex. It is also an often-misunderstood one. For example, both in the writing of the prophet Isaiah and in the New Testament epistle of James, Abraham is referred to as a "friend" of God.[6] It is even believed that the southern gate to the old city of Jerusalem has been known historically as the Friendship Gate in honor of the relationship between Abraham and God.[7] Supposedly, this tradition of thinking of God and Abraham as friends dates back to the middle of the third century to the first complete Greek version of the Old Testament known as the Septuagint [sep-two-a-gent]. The Septuagint translation of the verse reads, "The LORD said, 'Shall I hide from Abraham, my friend, what I am about to do?'" The phrase "my friend" does not exist in the original Hebrew, but the words were added for some reason by the translators. We know this because older translations that do not contain this reference have been found. It also makes sense to my students that this was an error. This God was no friend of Abraham! One student's question pretty much sums up all the questions I have received from this story. The student rhetorically asked, "Why would Abraham do what God told him to do? God hadn't been that great to him up to this point! After he killed his son, God was probably going to kill him anyway."

One must admit that the God of Abraham doesn't seem like much of a blessing to Abraham. Let's look at the record: On God's command, Abraham's first act as tribal leader after the death of his father, Terah, was to uproot his family and move them from what is present-day Iraq to Canaan, modern-day Israel. The journey surely took months, and it must have been a tremendous blow when, shortly after their arrival in Canaan, the family had to abandon the land because of a drought. Their only hope for survival was to flee south to Egypt and beg for food and water until the drought passed.

The details of their life in Egypt are not recorded, but one can imagine the severity of the circumstances. The irony is that this famine and the complete uprooting of his family come only a few verses after God promises Abraham the land. Genesis leaves us with a haunting image:

> Now there was a famine in the land. So Abram went down to Egypt to reside there as an alien, for the famine was severe in the land. (Gen. 12:10)

Life as an "alien" in Egypt surely wasn't easy. Abraham, for instance, so feared for his life, lest the Egyptians fancy his wife and kill him for her, that he schemed to protect himself and concomitantly improve his position by having Sarah represent herself as his sister. As the brother of a beautiful woman, Abraham could be bought off instead of being killed off as an inconvenient husband.[8] However clever he might have been, the image is not flattering of Father Abraham conniving to secure his temporary welfare by "selling" his wife into a harem. Curiously, my students generally don't blame Abraham for this, as they suppose that both he and Sarah did the best they could under the circumstances imposed on them by God. They may understand Abraham and Sarah; it is their God they find perplexing.

Ironically, it is the Pharaoh who acted most nobly in this story. When Pharaoh found out about Abraham's deception, he was repulsed by the man and his actions:

> "Why did you not tell me that she was your wife? Why did you say, 'She is my sister,' so that I took her for my wife? Now then, here is your wife, take her, and be gone." (Gen. 12:18–19)

Abraham's problems continued after the famine eased. On the way back to Canaan, there was trouble within the tribe. The family of Lot, Abraham's brother's son and closest surviving family member, had an angry disagreement with the rest of the company. The "discord"[9] ended in Abraham splitting the tribe. It seemed at every turn, Abraham did what he had to in order to survive. No matter the circumstances, he continued to believe that if he was loyal to God, great things would happen. He hoped to be vindicated—not judged by history to be a crazy old man hearing voices, but rather a faithful tribal leader and follower of God. One big obstacle stood in the way of fulfilling his dream: Abraham couldn't be father to a great nation without a child.

When finally back in Canaan, Abraham decided to take matters into his own hands. If God wouldn't give him a child, the culture in which he now lived had a solution. The Canaanites allowed for a surrogate wife, a handmaiden who could bear a child on behalf of a barren wife. His wife at first agreed to this strange arrangement and a child, Ishmael, was born to the surrogate mother. Under Canaanite law this child could "legally" be claimed as the child of Abraham. However, the system carried a heavy interpersonal price. The emotional strain was too much on Sarah, especially after the younger woman became pregnant with Abraham's child and "showed contempt" for Sarah. So, Sarah exerted a great deal of pressure on Abraham, and eventually he agreed to send away the child and the slave-mother. But the loss of Ishmael broke his heart. He not only lost the boy, it seemed he lost God's promise.

For Abraham, following the commands of his God was not easy. One is reminded of Tevye's line when he speaks to God in *Fiddler on the Roof*: "I know we are your chosen people, but couldn't you choose somebody else once in a while?"

An issue that confounds my students is why an all-knowing God doesn't know certain things. For example, why doesn't God know that Abraham would do whatever God asked him to do? Although we are relieved at the end of the story of the binding of Isaac when the boy is saved by the angel, we are left to wonder why Abraham was put through this potentially deadly exercise in the first place.

> "Do not lay your hand on the boy or do anything to him; for now I know that you fear God, since you have not withheld your son, your only son, from me." (Gen. 22:12)

The story of Abraham on Mt. Moriah is powerful and complex. It is well known by scholars as a passage difficult to interpret. However, for parents, the key to understanding the importance of this story first requires understanding its historical context.

Why Was a Sacrifice to God Necessary?

We know the Canaanites during the time of Abraham had an active worship system that centered on fertility rites. They were farmers and thus had an understandable preoccupation with the weather. In modern Israel, the land is green and bountiful because the Israelis use modern farming techniques and sophisticated irrigation systems. The ancient inhabitants of that land knew nothing of these methods; they had to scratch a living from a hostile soil. They felt they were at the mercy of climatological whimsy that only the gods could control.

These gods were called the Baalim, and they controlled the fertility of the land. These gods were headed by *Baal* [often pronounced "bail"], who was the storm god, the god of rain. Although there are only derogatory references to *Baal* in the Bible, this god had a powerful effect on the people of the region, including Abraham's clan. *Baal* had a consort, called by various names, including *Ashtoreth*. When, at his whim, *Baal* chose to fertilize the ground, his consort, the earth, brought forth life. Conversely, when there was drought or flood, the people reasoned that they had not pleased *Baal*. The worship of *Baal* was an old custom in the region and may have even pre-dated the Canaanite people of Abraham's day.

In contrast, Abraham's God was revealed through historical events. Canaan was, in Abraham's day, a crossroads of cultures where many gods were worshiped. Abraham may not have seen any conflict in worshiping his God as well as the local gods. After all, his God never claimed to be a farmer's god! Nor did his God, at this point, claim to be the only god. Even in the next book of the Bible, when the Israelites were saved from the water of the sea on their escape from Egypt, Moses and the Israelites sang, "Who is like you, O LORD, among the gods?" (Exod. 15:11).

When there is drought in America, we cringe because we know our fresh produce will be more expensive because it will have to come from another part of the world. Our modern food-delivery system is a luxury and a relatively new phenomenon. In the ancient world, life was more tenuous. If it didn't rain, or if it rained too much at the wrong time, famine came and people died. The Canaanites, like all people, desired to control the weather. It was commonly thought that some control of the weather as well as other events affecting the lives of the people were possible through the sacrificial system designed to please *Baal*.

At the heart of any system of sacrifice is the hope of getting something in return. What one wanted from a god dictated what one sacrificed. In a worship system based on sacrifice, what is received in response to a sacrifice is determined by the quality and the frequency of the supplicant's offering. In the case of *Baal*, the level of titillation was considered. In fertility rite systems, it was not unusual for a sexual act to be performed as part of a ritual designed to stimulate the fertility god into action. The supplicant, through his participation in the system, acknowledged the power of the deity and his dependence upon the god.[10] It does not require an extraordinary intellectual leap to imagine that if the sacrifice of a mere animal might move a deity, wouldn't the sacrifice of a child bring great blessings?

Human sacrifice has appeared from time to time in many ancient cultures, but few have ultimately incorporated the heinous practice as part of accepted worship. In the Bible, animal sacrifice was an accepted part of the worship of God into the time of the prophets. Even in the time of Jesus, an elaborate drainage system was engineered by the Romans for the second temple to provide for the efficient removal of the animal blood, a by-product of the daily sacrifices. Ritual sacrifice, in fact, was a common part of most religious worship and celebration in the ancient world. Even the God of the Christian gospel had to offer a son as a sacrifice and expiation for our sins. As Paul writes:

> For there is no distinction, since all have sinned and fall short of the glory of God; they are now justified by [God's] grace as a gift, through the redemption that is in Christ Jesus, whom God put forward as a sacrifice of atonement by [God's] blood, effective through faith. (Rom. 3:22–25)

If God found it necessary to permit the sacrifice of Jesus in order to end the requirement of sacrifice for all time, we must look at Abraham's plans for Isaac with more sympathetic eyes. Jesus was the final sacrifice. His crucifixion ended all sacrifice. But in Abraham's world, a sacrifice sufficient to show the depth of his love for God required the supreme act.

A View from Mt. Moriah

Even when we understand Abraham's world, the story of the binding of Isaac appalls us. We are left to wonder what kind of man would consider such a thing. What kind of god would require it?

Isaac innocently asks when they arrive at the place of sacrifice: "The fire and the wood are here, but where is the lamb for a burnt offering?" (Gen. 22:7). Abraham must have been tempted to lie. I remember in a far less dramatic moment when my daughter was four-years-old and I sat in the hospital emergency room waiting for the doctor to set her badly fractured arm.

She asked, "Will it hurt?" When I told her, "Yes, it will hurt," I could see her face get a little older. I remember a friend telling me about a question his dying young son had asked him. After months of powerful drugs and painful procedures to reduce a tumor that pressed on vital areas of the brain, his son was getting no better. When his son asked him, "Am I going to die?" all the father could do was cry. The father could not speak the truth to his son because to say the words brought the truth closer to reality. We can wonder if Abraham chose to lie to Isaac instead of telling his only son the truth. Could Abraham not bear to look at Isaac's face and tell him what God wanted him to do?

Mt. Moriah is a good place to have a religious experience. Today, the Mt. Moriah in Abraham's account is part of the Temple Mount in the city of Jerusalem held sacred by Muslims, Jews, and Christians. When Abraham stood there, however, it was barren. Alone with his son, away from those with whom he had traveled, Abraham was about to make one of the most important decisions of his life: to trust God again.

It is possible that some code was buried in God's command. Perhaps, Abraham thought that to "offer" his son would be all that was necessary. Even during the time of Jesus, the child of a Jew was symbolically offered to God and purchased back in a temple ritual signifying that the child belonged to God and was merely placed in the family's trust. We are not told that Abraham had such confidence. All Abraham can say to his son is: "The LORD will provide . . ." (Gen. 22:14). The word *provide* in Latin means "to see" or "to have vision." So what Abraham is saying to his son is a statement of faith. He is saying, I can't see what God is doing, but I trust God. Abraham had confidence in God even when God's command was incomprehensible.

A student of mine once observed that perhaps Abraham's real act of faith was that he *didn't* kill Isaac! My student reasoned that if Abraham lived in a culture that accepted human sacrifice as an extraordinary expression of religious devotion, then perhaps some really important occasion in Abraham's life or in the life of his family or the people with whom he lived necessitated this sacrifice. This occasion might have been something the Genesis writer didn't know about. If this was the case, the planned sacrifice of Isaac was a desperate religious act aimed at getting his God to intervene in some crisis. To return home without completing the act would make him the subject of scorn and possible retribution from his neighbors.

My student had hit on one of the theories about sacrifice that Edward Norbeck explains in his book, *Religion in Primitive Society.* He writes:

One of the ways of men to win the good will of other men is to endear themselves by valuable and, if the occasion warrants, precious gifts, and human life is often if not always precious.[11]

Abraham had already endured famine, personal humiliation, and family crisis. Was this situation worse than those? Or was he simply so beaten at this point in his life that he decided to face this new, unnamed crisis the way a Canaanite would?

No one knows. The power of this story is that it invites us into this dark moment and doesn't give us a clue about what to expect next. We do know that in desperate times, desperate people do desperate things.

A Parent's Faith in God

And he believed the LORD; and the LORD reckoned it to him as righteousness. (Gen. 15:6)

"God himself will provide . . ." (Gen. 22:8)

The two verses we have discussed from the story of Abraham form the foundation of the faith a parent must place in God. Abraham knew that faith in God required a belief that God would be present even when God couldn't be seen. As the writer of Hebrews expressed it: "Now faith is the assurance of things hoped for, the conviction of things not seen" (Heb. 11:1).

Abraham may have gone to Mt. Moriah, dazed and confused by circumstances at home, desperate to do something extraordinary to move his God to act in a situation. But, despite his desperation, despite the abhorrent act he was contemplating, God turned it into something good. God, Abraham believed, would change his actions from that of a religious fanatic to a positive moral act of faith, and God did not let him down.

Abraham achieved a transcendent perspective only by first placing his faith in the biblical God. Once he placed his faith in God, even the tremendous cultural pressures he endured were no match. God was faithful to Abraham once Abraham placed his faith in God. We can believe that just as God was faithful to Abraham, God will be faithful to us.

Martin Luther grasped the central point of the Abraham story:

When the Divine Majesty thinks about me that I am righteous . . . then I am truly righteous, not through my works but through faith, with which I grasp the divine thought.[12]

Parents can't always see the way clearly when we are making decisions about our children. I remember a father who made an appointment to come see me. The message I received said it was an extremely important matter. When the man arrived, I could tell he was agitated. He told me he had been thinking about this problem for months and now felt at his wits end. His son would be graduating in just a few months, and upon his eighteenth birthday that summer, the boy would inherit $20 million. A trust fund set up by the boy's grandfather had grown exponentially and was now larger than anyone had anticipated. The father had known of the trust but had no idea of its size until very recently. What should he do? He had already checked with the attorneys, and he learned that the trust could not be broken, and that all the money would pass to the boy in a lump sum.

I had no advice for the man. The die was cast. All he could do was have faith that the values he had taught his son would carry the boy through this coming avalanche of temptation. However, I have often wished I had the presence of mind to retell this father the story of Abraham. Abraham had to do what he surely must have known was wrong, perform an act he hated. Abraham trusted God to take care of his child, and all parents are called to the same faith. Modern parents seem to prefer to control and plan our children's lives thinking that because we love them, we should be able to break them out of the chrysalis of childhood. Butterflies freed from their birth container by an outside force never develop the strength to fly on their own. Christian parents must believe that if we give our children the seed, they can grow their own faith, one perhaps stronger and more enduring than ours. Faith in God will lead our children to righteousness and goodness in God's good time. Parents must be patient and trust God. We are called to the faith the psalmist holds before us:

> Wait for the LORD;
>   be strong, and let your
> heart take courage;
> wait for the LORD!
>   (Ps. 27:14)

Even when we cannot see the way, God sees! We must believe that the angel sent by God to hold back the knife of Abraham will be sent to us if we make the wrong decisions about our children or about our lives. Justin Martyr believed this, and it brought him courage. Abraham believed this, and it saved his son. We can believe it too; God will not let us down.

My mother had Alzheimer's. As the disease progressed and the parent-child roles reversed, my sister and I fretted many times that we were not doing the right thing for Mother. In the early stages, she was, at times, irascible; then, at other times, she was more like a confused and frightened child. We were never sure what would happen next, and often she resented what we decided to do for her. We constantly questioned ourselves. Were we overreacting? Would she be safe if we weren't more directive? These questions plagued us. However, at each turn, we chose faith and charged ahead like Abraham, praying for guidance, hoping for a miracle.

As it turned out, most of our decisions were for the best. The ones that we would do over haven't seemed to matter in the long run. I believe God took our good intentions and our faith and love of our mother and turned them into good. If we believe that Abraham walked to Mt. Moriah, taking each step believing that what he felt compelled to do would be transformed by God for good, then we see the real faith of Abraham.

It is not what we do for or what we give to our children that will be our most-enduring gifts to them; rather, our real gift will be to show them through our lives the transcendent perspective that comes through faith in God. We can give our children no greater gift than to show them our faith and to let them know that they can take this same faith to their Moriahs. We are invited by a loving God to walk into the future with our children and our faith, believing as Abraham did that all will be transformed to good by God.

Faith in Our Children

The second kind of faith parents must have is faith in our children. To have faith in a child, we must be willing to lose our child. Just as Mary and Joseph were called to do in the Temple, we are called to offer our child back to God. Letting go of a child, granting independence, allowing an increasing amount of distance between us, is very difficult. We love our children and want to protect them and keep them close. Being a parent would be easier if keeping our arms around our child was all we had to do. We would never let go. God knows this, so God has shown us what we must do. God has shown us how to lovingly withdraw from a child's life.

Parent *Absconditus*

God seems to grow more remote as we read through the Hebrew Bible. In theology, the gradual changing in the way God communicates with the characters of the Bible from the opening chapters of Genesis to the prophetic era, the way God seems to grow more distant, is called *Deus Absconditus* [the hiding or the hiddenness of God]. The phrase itself comes from "Truly, you are a God who hides himself, O God of Israel." (Isa. 45:15).

"God disappears in the Bible." With these extraordinary words, Professor Richard Elliot Friedman of the University of California, San Diego, began his very fine book, *The Disappearance of God.*[13]

> The Bible begins, as nearly everybody knows, with a world in which God is actively and visibly involved, but it does not end that way. Gradually through the course of the Hebrew Bible, the deity appears less and less to humans, speaks less and less. Miracles, angels, and all other signs of divine presence become rarer and finally cease. In the last portions of the Hebrew Bible, God is not present in the well-known apparent ways of the earlier books. Among God's last words to Moses, the deity says, "I will hide my face from them. I shall see what their end will be." (Deut. 31:17–18, 32:20). By the end of the story, God does just that.[14]

Friedman carefully documents the changing relationship of Yahweh and creation. He notes that in the garden, God is heard walking in the "cool of the day." The anthropomorphic image of God, a very human-like portrayal of God strolling as if on equal terms with Adam and Eve, is in stark contrast to the abstract image of the God just one book later in the story of the burning bush. Friedman writes,

> The great burst of miracles that fills the first half of Exodus is depicted explicitly as "signs," evidences of Yahweh's involvement in the world; Yahweh declares that [God] causes a plague to happen in a particular way "in order that you will know that I, Yahweh, am in the midst of the earth" (Exodus 8:18,cf. 7:17; 8:6; 9:14, 29).[15]

Then things change. In a powerfully revealing passage in the middle of the book of Exodus, the whole relationship changes as the people, terrified after having "witnessed the thunder and lightning, the sound of the trumpet, and the mountain smoking . . ." (Exod. 20:18), say to Moses, "You speak to us, and we will listen; but do not let God speak to us, or we will die" (vs.19). Friedman notes, "After this scene in the Bible, Yahweh never again speaks directly to an entire community Himself."[16] Not only is the relationship between God and God's creation changed after this moment, but a new phenomenon is introduced: prophecy. The prophets use existing signs, images, and visions to convey God's message. Friedman traces this trend through the time of the Judges and writes:

> From the beginning of the Bible to this point in the narrative, the deity has been said to have appeared to Abraham, Isaac, Jacob (Exod 6:3),

Moses, Joshua (Deut 31:15), Aaron (Lev 16:2), Israel (Lev 9:4; Num 14:14), Samuel (I Sam 3:21), David (2 Chr 3:1), and Solomon. But now, with about five centuries of the story still to be told in the Hebrew Bible, the deity has appeared to a human being for the last time.[17]

The immediate response of the Christian might be, "But oh, you are wrong, Professor Friedman. God is not gone. This absence is only temporary, for in the New Testament God is present with us in God's son Jesus and in the power of the Holy Spirit."

Friedman judiciously addresses the messiahship of Jesus by putting a fine point on his argument. Even in the Gospels ". . . God the father, God as known in the Hebrew Bible—remains hidden."[18]

God's withdrawal from familiar relationships with Adam and Abraham is not neglect or disinterest. God's love doesn't change, but God is present in the lives of the characters of the Bible in a very different way. By God's example as our divine parent, God is giving parents an example to follow. To rear healthy and appropriately independent children is to engage in a systematic and loving process of withdrawing from the child's life. Looking closely at the biblical account, we see that God withdraws in a very special way, for God withdraws while remaining powerfully present in the lives of God's children.

The best parents I have known have exercised their faith in their children through their thoughtful and loving withdrawal. Each new developmental stage requires different efforts on the part of parents. These parents knew that without a conscious effort to give a child more distance, a child cannot grow strong and resilient. We must have faith in our children and in God's example, for when we find ways of withdrawing as God did, paradoxically, our ties to our children grow stronger. A few examples might help.

Perry's Story

One evening I received a call from a friend. He wanted to apologize and said that he and his wife would be unable to come for dinner the following Friday because he had forgotten a commitment they had made some time ago. He sheepishly said, "You will laugh when you hear what I have forgotten. Two months ago, we said we would chaperone a middle school dance."

I did laugh, and told him that I would be thinking of him on Friday evening. He said he was dreading the whole thing. He assured me he wanted to get out of it because his son was upset that he and his wife would be present at the dance. The boy had not known his parents had volunteered and was furious when he saw the chaperone list at school. The boy threatened not to go and made life miserable at home as he anticipated his parents' embarrassing presence at the dance. He would never live it down!

My friend told his son that he was sorry this whole event upset him but that he and his wife had made a promise to the school and intended to keep their word. He did say, rather woefully, that he was willing to accept a last-minute dispensation from the headmaster. However, none was offered.

Sometime later I saw my friend and asked how the dance had gone. He said, "To my surprise, we had a wonderful evening." However, it didn't start off that way. The boy acceded to going to the dance; however, the drive to school was marked by angry explosions from his son. When they arrived at the dance, a faculty member, sensing the situation, stationed these parents outside. Their jobs were to ensure that no uninvited guests came into the function. The first part of the evening was uneventful, but soon, my friend reported, his son appeared outside. Not once, but several times. The boy returned periodically throughout the evening just to talk. He even brought some of his friends out to meet his parents. My friend concluded with astonishment that, after all the hysteria, "Perry actually seemed glad we were there. We all had a great time!"

This is a good example of wise parents' *absconditus*. As children grow, they want increased distance from their parents, but because they have never been adolescents before, they mistakenly ask for our absence. We need to know what our children are really asking. By withdrawing in a thoughtful and appropriate way, we tell our children that we both love them and respect their growing more independent. By allowing them to take steady strides toward their freedom in our presence, we give them the message that we have faith in them.

There is no magical formula for exercising *absconditus*, but there is no need for a psychology degree, either. It is usually just a matter of adults using common sense and remembering God's example in Scripture. A healthy long-term relationship with a child is based on a commitment on the part of the parent to honor and to encourage the child's growing independence.

Preschool Lessons

Independence means that both the parent and the child must be willing to take some chances. I remember one time when my daughter was only two years old, and I took her to an opening-school picnic. This picnic was for the families of all the new preschoolers who would start school the next day. The playground was familiar to my daughter. Although my child was too young to attend preschool, my wife and I would regularly take her to the playground. The evening of the picnic she was delighted to see other children present when we arrived for the festivities. The very first thing she did was to head to her favorite place, the "fort," a large wooden structure (nick-named by the Board of Trustees "Fort Liability") with its large red tubular slide. The other children had discovered it too. They formed a line and moved orderly up the stairs, along the walkway, and down the slide.

The agility of the three- and four-year-olds far exceeded that of my two-year-old, and soon the older children were growing impatient with my daughter's clumsy mounting of the stairs and shifting to the slide. They began to brush her aside and move onto the slide. She frequently lost her balance and would sit down hard because a larger child, two years her senior, had unintentionally bumped her.

Although this happened many years ago, I remember it very clearly as one of my first tests of needing to give my child some independence. From my perch with the other parents not far away from the fort, I could see that she was having trouble. Her initial laughter as the older kids bumped her and pushed her out of the way quickly turned to frustration, and tears welled. She looked at me.

I knew in a few days I would be addressing the parents of these children in their first meeting as new parents at the school. Among other introductory items, I would be preparing them for some of the distance that would need to be created between them and their children in order for the school to do its work. The preschool teachers always joke that tears were spilled twice on the first day of school. First, parents cried in the morning when they dropped off their children, and then the children cried at the end of school when they had to go home.

I didn't respond to my daughter's appeal. I did let her know I was looking at her, but I made it clear that I wasn't going to interfere. I tried to convey that I had faith in her and her ability to handle the situation. I encouraged her by gesture to get up and keep trying. It may have looked like a small matter to the casual observer, but, in reality, the self-restraint I exercised took everything that I could muster. She was safe, I reminded myself. She didn't really need me to interfere; rather, she needed me to temporarily withdraw but remain a reassuring distance away.

By adopting this principle of *absconditus* in our parenting and reminding ourselves of it during each of the stages through which our children grow, we can give them the clear message that our love for them is like God's love for all of us. We will love them in such a way that our love never stands between them and growing up. That day both my daughter and her father learned a lot.

Calls from College

Not so long ago, I fell into conversation with a mother of a young graduate of my school. The girl was now at the end of her first year of college, and I inquired how the mother thought things had gone. The report was glowing, and I heard the things any head of school loves to hear. The mother was highly complimentary of both her daughter's preparation for college and the college counseling process that had helped select a college just right for her daughter's needs. In the midst of the conversation, the mother made an interesting observation. She said, "I didn't know it was going to be this hard being a parent when they got to college."

The comment interested me, so I asked for more specifics. The mother told me she had been forced to insist that her daughter not come home as often as the girl wanted. Very social in high school, the daughter had purposely selected a small college without a great deal of weekend activity so that she might have fewer distractions from her work. The plan was producing the desired effect. Serious effort was producing good grades, but the desire to visit home kept popping up in the regular telephone calls the parents received.

At one point, the girl had the flu and cried over the telephone for permission to come home to recuperate. The mother told me that saying "no" to that request was one of the hardest things she had ever had to do as a parent. She had to go against her instincts as a mother to do what was right as a parent. She said she knew her daughter was getting the necessary attention from the college infirmary. Getting over the flu on one's own was part of growing up. They both cried together on the telephone, but the right decision was made and the girl stayed at college. Real maturity was being reached in small steps.

Good Night, Dad

A loving father once told me of his *absconditus*. I learned from him that knowing what to stop doing as a parent is as important as knowing what to do. He told me of a small ritual he observed every day. From the day his daughter came home from the hospital, he tucked her into bed each night, and he rarely missed their evening prayer together. He said he would say a blessing and they would exchange a few words about the day. He told me that he knew the daily event was far more important to him than to his daughter, especially as she grew into her early teenage years, but she indulged him and he was grateful.

One evening as he made his way up the stairs to her room, he heard his daughter call through the closed door of her room, "Good night, Dad." He said he knew exactly what she meant. Her tone was not angry, merely emphatic. She wanted to end the ritual; she was too old for her father's "Good night."

He bid her a good night from the stairs and went outside to sit on the deck. There he began to cry. He knew a chapter in his parenting was over; he knew it was time for him to give up the little ritual that had meant so much to him. He was profoundly sad. He cried alone that evening, never telling his daughter or his wife how sad he was. But, he knew another father would understand. As we sat in the restaurant talking, our eyes moistened. His tears were because he was still sad, mine were because my daughter was only a few years younger than his at the time and I knew my turn would soon come. I hoped I would have his same good sense.

As the years passed, I got my turn. One evening when I passed my teenage daughter in the kitchen I startled her by giving her a hug. I often did this when she was younger, but since she had become "cool," I usually kept my distance. The gesture confused her momentarily and she hugged me back. Then, regaining her composure, she pushed me away, appalled that she had let down her guard. She quickly and haughtily sallied out of the kitchen, but not before she tossed some sage advice over her shoulder: "Dad, why don't you get a dog?"

Grandma Knows Best

Grandparents can often help us. I remember a grandmother telling me of a time when she received a call from the nurse at the summer camp her grandson attended. She lived near the camp and was the person designated to call in an emergency. The camp nurse was clear when she called the grandmother that there was no emergency, but her grandson was very upset and was complaining of a stomachache. It was late and the other boys were off in their cabins.

The grandmother drove to the camp and got the boy. He wasn't sick, just extremely homesick. He had tried to fight his feelings during the first few days of camp, but to no avail. He wanted to leave the camp.

After a sandwich and some soup, the grandmother assured herself that there was no medical problem underlying the boy's complaints. She also knew leaving the camp would be a setback for her grandson, who was slow to develop independence. She put the boy to bed.

At 5:00 A.M. she awakened him. "I think we should go back to camp now," she told him. "You can be back in bed before any of the boys know you were gone." The boy went back and stayed the full term. During that session of camp, he learned more than how to paddle a canoe.

"Let This Cup Pass"

One of the most powerful scenes in the Bible occurs when Jesus is praying in the garden before his arrest. Jesus was not only fully human when he asked for the "cup" to pass from him but also fully a child with a parent powerful enough to change events. Even though his "cup" would lead to the cross, God did not intervene. God allowed Jesus to face the events before him because God knew the great triumph that awaited him and the great gift Jesus would be to the world.

The *absconditus* of God, captured in Scripture, should not be confused with neglect. God did not abandon Jesus nor does our God ever abandon us. Rather, God withdrew in such a way that all the characters in the Bible grew stronger and more confident.

Vainglory: A Parent's Sin

A parent's inability to model God's behavior when it comes to a systematic and loving withdrawal from a child's life causes a child to both struggle harder for independence and to struggle against the parent. This struggle creates an impossible situation for the child. Instead of the parent aiding the child, a bad parent becomes an obstacle. This is the sin of vainglory.

Ralph Wood of Baylor University sees vainglory as a societywide preoccupation. He observed this phenomenon as " . . . telling one's own story as if it were God's story."[19] Vainglory is our wish to occupy as large a place in another's mind as we occupy in our own. Of course, this is not possible. The other person is so full of thoughts of himself, he cannot give us as much room in his mind as we would like. But, we try anyway to impress ourselves on another, only to be disappointed and discouraged. When this happens in an adult/adult relationship, often a ruinous cycle begins. However, this desire on the part of a parent for glory in a child's mind leads to one of the most frequent and most destructive mistakes of parenting.

In the elementary school years, the sun can rise and set on a teacher in a child's eyes. Glorious reports of good behavior from teachers can stand in marked contrast to the same child's actions at home. The child's willingness to perform for teachers but not for us can rankle any parent. However, a child's broadening of sources of authority in her life is a natural development. It is the desire to keep that child devoted only to us that starts us down the road to the sin of vainglory.

I knew a single divorced mother who had grown so dependent on the approbation of her child that, as the child became more involved in school activities in the middle school years and less interested in the mother's smothering domination of her, the mother concocted a reason to take the child out of school for a long period of international travel. The child and mother traveled alone. Forced to come home by legal action from the child's father, the mother arranged for the child to enroll in a school seventy miles away from her home. Each day, she drove her child past dozens of schools to travel to and from the distant school. The staggering daily distance ensured limited after-school activities, isolation from local peers, and hours of exclusive time with mother. This was full-blown vainglory.

One of the most insightful writers I have found on this particular deadly parent behavior wasn't a parent. In fact, he was a monk who lived in the fourth century. His teaching on what he called the "Eight Deadly Thoughts" is enormously helpful in every area, but particularly here. His name was Evagrius[20] [E-vag-re-us] and he taught that we can avoid the deadly thoughts that lead to any sin, but we must first be willing to expose the deadly thoughts for what they are. We must be honest with ourselves to avoid sin. Both Jesus and Evagrius saw the thought of a sin being as morally powerful as the act of the sin itself. However, between the thought and the action lies the crucial moment of decision. In that moment, both public morality and most of parenting are lived. Jesus taught us, "I say to you that everyone who looks at a woman with lust has already committed adultery with her in his heart" (Matt. 5:28). Evagrius put it this way:

> Now it is essential to understand these matters so that when these various evil thoughts set. . . to work we are in a position to address effective words against them. . . those words which correctly characterize the one present. And we must do this before they drive us out of our state of mind.[21]

The "state of mind," of which Evagrius writes is our thinking when we are closest to God in our daily life. Sinful thoughts must be exposed and, with that disclosure, the deadly thoughts can be prevented from turning into evil work. The words that expose the demons are the words of truth, truth about ourselves. These words must be spoken no matter how painful the revelation is. Just as in John Bunyan's *Pilgrim's Progress*,[22] when the central character, the intrepid Christian, is locked in the dungeon and he thinks there is no hope for escape from the monster who will devour him, he is reminded that the key to the lock of his prison is in his pocket. Like Bunyan, Evagrius thought that we need only reach within ourselves to find the key that God has given us to the locks of our own deadly thoughts. With that key, we can then expose these thoughts and, thus, free ourselves from their power over us.

෯෯෯෯෯

Many children in this world are in danger. Most of them are easy to find. They live in poverty, are underfed, neglected, and often abused. They are not, however, the only children in danger. Some children who are in danger live in fine houses. They do not want for food or medical care, but they are developing an increasing sense of hopelessness because they are prevented from growing strong. Much of the senseless violence and self-destructive behavior committed by children who live in relative comfort is tied to their desperate attempts to be free. Some parents seem to want to take back God's gift of freedom, trying in vain to protect their children from the consequences of their behavior. Scott Peck, in *The Road Less Traveled*, makes the insightful observation that ". . . when we avoid the legitimate suffering that results from dealing with problems, we also avoid the growth that problems demand from us."[23] Without some experience with suffering, without some emotional resiliency gained from the experience of small failures in childhood, our children will be ill-equipped to live successfully.

Children must learn to cope with setbacks in order to lead happy lives as adults. In triumphing over the challenges of childhood and adolescence, they learn that the sun will come up the next morning and that life will go on. In contrast, the child who has been taught that life must be without disappointment, that he must be rewarded lavishly for the smallest accomplishment, that any defeat is a kind of death, and that he cannot succeed without someone's help or be happy without constant approbation, is the child who looks for a gun when things aren't going his way.

Ten Things a Parent Can Tell a Child
to Help Him/Her See Things God's Way

1. We live in a world that glorifies sentimentality. God is sometimes confused with a "good feeling." Tell your children that God is much more than this. God is a power that changes the way we see things.

2. Even good people can do bad things when they are separated from God.

3. If God is not in our life, we can accomplish no lasting good.

4. There is no lasting value system without God.

5. Acquiring a transcendent perspective on life, the eyes of our divine parent requires hard work, study, and prayer.

6. The purpose of religion is to tie us to God and to one another. Good religion unites people for good. Bad religion divides people and preaches hate.

7. What we believe shapes our actions. When we believe in God, God takes our failures and makes them holy.

8. It's OK to argue with God. Abraham did. But, when we argue with God, we must be ready to listen to God's response.

9. God knows what we need. We pray to learn what we really need.

10. We will give you more distance because we love you, but we will stay in your life for the same reason.

Chapter 4

Truth: The Absolute Horizon

I know a loving father who is divorced. At the time of this story, both of his children were under the age of eight. His wife's request that he leave the house was a shock to him, and the subsequent divorce was emotionally hard on him. Living away from his children, whom he loved very much, deeply troubled him. When I saw him just after the divorce was final, we talked about his return to single life and the challenges of being a weekend dad, a routine the court had imposed on him. I asked how the children were adjusting. He said they were doing well, but he feared that despite the active role he was trying to play in their daily lives, they were catching on to the fact that he and their mother were divorced. "You haven't told them?" I asked incredulously. He said he thought they were too young to upset them with the news.

Keeping the truth from children at any age is wrong and dangerous. Children deserve the whole truth, but it should be delivered in a box they can lift.

A young mother told me of a disappointing encounter with her child. She was stuck on how to proceed and wondered if I had any advice. Her three-year-old daughter had asked the question parents dread, "Where do babies come from?" The mother was committed to telling her daughter the truth. She showed the child pictures of the fallopian tube and tried to explain the path and mobility of the sperm, but the child's reaction was not what she had hoped. "Yuck," was the child's response. "I think I over did it," the mother confessed.

To tell the truth to children, parents must first gauge what the child wants to know. The best way to find that out is to ask the child. The answer will contain clues needed for the next step. If the mother had simply asked the child, "What is it you want to know about how babies are made?" she would have had a more successful discussion with her child. One aspect of the birth process that often captures the imagination of young children is, "How did the baby get in the mommy?" This is not usually a question about sexual intercourse, but rather a very concrete question. Fortunately, there are good books available for young children that can serve as an adequate follow-up to their initial question. However, despite what educational aids are used, the principle always remains the same: The wise parent tells the truth to a child, choosing always to travel toward the truth at the child's pace. It is also important for children to be reassured that whatever the subject, our love for them includes an unshakeable willingness to tell them the truth.

Children are stronger than adults think. Often adults lie to children because we don't want to face the truth ourselves. The divorced father I referred to earlier was trying to keep the news of the divorce from his children because he was still hoping for reconciliation with his wife. Unfortunately, he was not only kidding himself, he was running the risk of teaching his children that he didn't trust them with the truth.

When we tell a child that Spot really didn't die, but that the veterinarian sent him to a farm where he will be happy, we leave a child to wonder what was so wrong that the dog got sick. When the truth about the dog is found out, and it almost always is, power over the child has been put into the hands of those who will tell her the truth. A woman once told me that she was a teenager before she questioned a story her mother had told her years earlier about her dog's death. The question arose when she told a friend at school that her dog had died from the splinters it had gotten from sitting on a picnic bench. The friend laughed and said she had been told a lie. Upon her return from school, the teenager asked her mother for the truth. The truth was that the dog had distemper and had to be destroyed. The mother didn't want her young daughter to think the dog's odd behavior was due to a mental illness. Reflecting on her relationship with her mother, the woman told me this strange line of reasoning was "typical of my mother." This woman grew up knowing that she could not trust her mother to tell her the truth. The mother frequently chose some fantastic lie in the false hope of protecting her daughter from a truth she judged worse than the lie. What she got, however, was a teenager, and eventually a grown daughter, who always relied on others for the truth.

Children and Funerals

Parents often ask me at what age a child should be allowed to go to a grandparent's funeral. I always answer, "any age." Children have a right to see death and to watch adults grieve. This is how they learn appropriate ways of grieving. Without the truth about death, children can dream up worse things on their own. I know a mature woman who still speaks with great passion of her mother's decision not to allow her to attend her father's funeral. She was a young child in elementary school when her father died. She says she remembers not knowing what to feel after the event. All she was told was that her father was gone. She was excluded from all the events of the funeral. She says she imagined for years that she would someday see her father walking down the street. She also remembers not knowing what to say to her friends. They wanted to console her and talk to her about the event, but she had nothing to say because she knew nothing. She felt disloyal to her father. All she was left with were her conflicted feelings, confusion, and worry that she had somehow contributed to her father's death. She decided she had done something wrong and that was why her mother didn't want her at the funeral.

A death in the family is an emotional event, even when the death is anticipated. I counsel parents to give some thought ahead of time as to what they will say to their child before he actually attends the funeral services. The grave-side ceremony is as important as the church service for the child to attend. The "closure" of graveside begins the healing process.

The tradition of "viewing the body" presents another problem. Parents should be prepared for the concrete thinking of young children and the questions it will spawn. A parent told me about overhearing his six-year-old discussing his grandfather's death with a young cousin. The parent realized that he hadn't fully prepared his son for all the aspects of the funeral when he overheard the boy's conversation at the funeral home. Looking at the body in the casket, his son said, "My dad told me that grandpa died and went to heaven. But now he's back!"

Children must learn it is O.K. to be sad about the death of a loved one and that it is normal to grieve. Grief is also normal over the loss of a pet. Death doesn't scare a child nearly as much as not knowing the truth. We once had a stir in our preschool because Snowball died. Snowball was the preschool's rabbit. The children found it dead one morning. Of course, Snowball had previous lives. Usually when the fuzzy friend had gone on for his reward, he was quickly replaced overnight so he wasn't missed. This way, generations of preschoolers all enjoyed Snowball's presence. But his death, this time, came during the school day. So, the director of the preschool decided to have a funeral for Snowball. Off the three- and four-year-olds went to the woods. They spent the morning digging a hole (a very successful activity!), and all the children said their goodbyes to Snowball at the grave side. They fell silent when the body, wrapped in a towel, was covered with dirt. They planted flowers on the grave. After the burial, the children returned happily to school.

The preschool teachers each called or spoke directly to the parents of the children at the end of the day to explain what happened and to encourage them to talk to their children about the event. However, several of the parents were very upset. They wondered why we would scare the children in such a way. The teachers explained that the rabbit's death was not planned, but when the animal fell lifeless in the cage in front of the children, the teachers were not going to create a lie. The teachers explained to the children that Snowball's life was over. They answered their questions, and the children were fine; even the youngest child can understand that death is a part of life. It is better for children to learn life's truths from those who love them than from those who might not have their best interests at heart.

Santa Claus

"Hello" was the only word I said for the first several minutes of the telephone conversation. In the course of the following diatribe, I was asked a series of rhetorical questions: "How could you do such a thing?" and, "What kind of minister are you?" The point of the parent's anger was my presumption in referring to Santa Claus as a myth during a recent sermon to middle school students. This parent's daughter had told her of my reference in chapel, and the mother was furious with me. She assured me that until I had made the comment, her daughter believed in Santa Claus. Now that simple childhood joy had been taken away by the headmaster. It was clear to her that I didn't understand how difficult it was for parents to maintain a small sense of wonder in a ten-year-old's life. "They are just children!" she exclaimed. "The school and all of society want them to grow up too fast, why can't you let them be children?"

I was guilty of the reference, but I hadn't done anything wrong. The theme of my sermon her child had recounted had been integrity, and I was preaching on the text, "you have shown you are trustworthy in small things" (Matt. 25:21 NJB). My purpose was to link the school's student-run Honor Code to the biblical imperative to be trustworthy in the small things in life as a way of preparing oneself to be trustworthy in big things. Under our school's distinctively Jeffersonian Honor Code tradition, a student is not to lie, cheat, or steal. I drew a parallel in my chapel sermon between the tradition of the Honor Code and the teachings of Jesus.

No matter my intentions, the illustration was what had gotten me in trouble with this mother. I had mentioned that if adults and older siblings were going to ask young children to incorporate a high standard of integrity into their lives, we all needed to be careful about the messages we gave children.

I stated that parents and other well-meaning adults and siblings make a mistake when they continue the Santa Claus myth well beyond the age when it is appropriate (about six-years-old) because it gives conflicting messages to children. It is important for a child to build a trusting relationship with adults and older brothers and sisters. We say, "Trust me in great things, but with little things like Santa Claus and the Easter Bunny, let's keep playing a game." For the young child, however, Santa's existence is *not* a small thing.

In our culture, I see an absurd infantilization of young people, especially at Christmastime, bribing them to participate in a game they know is for the entertainment of adults. Look closely into the eyes of the next ten-year-old you have asked, "What did Santa bring you this year?" Unless your tongue was planted firmly in your cheek (for the ten-year-old is capable of enjoying many adult conventions of speech and "in jokes"), you will see a child "playing the lie" when she decides that it is time to get on with the little charade she assumes the adults want her to play.

The communication parents seek with their teenagers is lost not in the great mysteries of puberty, but in the small lies they told the children earlier in life. When children are wise enough to know that the chimney flue couldn't possibly accommodate a person, let alone a jolly fat man, the game is over. It is a mistake to prolong the charade beyond that point. If we do, we run the risk of giving a message to our young children that they will be rewarded for playing a little game of deception with us. Once we have introduced an acceptable level of deceit, lying becomes easier. Children quickly understand that the lies parents tell them are intended to control their behavior. They intuitively understand what Jesus had to explain to his adult disciples: When you know the truth, "the truth will make you free" (John 8:32). Perhaps that is why some teenagers struggle so hard to escape their parents; they know they have to get away to get the truth.

When I have spoken about this issue to groups of parents, I am always asked how parents know when it is time to tell children the truth about such things as Santa, the Easter Bunny, and the Tooth Fairy. I tell them that if they really listen, their children will tell them.

The Tooth Fairy

My daughter once confided a secret in me when she was five-and-a-half years old. One summer night when I was putting her to bed shortly after she had lost one of her baby teeth, she tested me with: "I know Mommy is the Tooth Fairy."

"Oh? Why do you think that?"

"I pretended I was asleep when she came in the room to take my tooth from under the pillow."

"Maybe you were dreaming?" I suggested as I busied myself with the evening routine, hoping for a distraction to arise to take us away from the subject. "No, because she dropped it and I still have it," she said nonchalantly.

I was afraid she knew that I was an accomplice in the Tooth Fairy caper, for surely she had seen me crawling around her bedroom floor in the dark looking for the tooth after my wife had reported it missing. My wife had carefully exchanged the tooth for the Susan B. Anthony silver dollar in the special pouch hidden under my daughter's sleeping head. But she dropped it. After a sometimes noisy search of the floor around the bed on our hands and knees, we still could not find the tooth! Apparently my daughter had discovered it and was keeping it as evidence.

"I think you're Santa Claus too," she pressed.

"Oh? And how have you come to think that?"

No response.

"If you don't want to believe in Santa Claus, that's all right," I said to her in my most psychological tone.

"Well, I know that you buy all the toys, and Mom wraps them," she challenged.

"So," I responded too quickly. "Even Santa needs a little help." However, I could feel myself getting defensive. Was I going to be the one grandmother would hate for ruining Christmas?

"You know, sweetheart, maybe you are right," I rallied. "After all, I love you, and I'm sure Santa loves you. I like to give you presents, and so does he; but, I have just one little girl to love and he has so many. Maybe I am *your* Santa Claus?" She smiled and said, "Oh, Daddy," in that dismissive way of the young.

I am happy to report that Christmas at our house went along merrily despite this discovery. The excitement of Christmas was as palpable as ever; however, we just stopped pretending that Santa Claus brought the little surprises left under the tree. After Santa Claus was put in his place, Christmas took on a more thoughtful tone. We were free to talk more about the real meaning of Christmas. We made only one rule for our daughter: If any younger children ask her, "Is Santa Claus real?" she is to tell them to talk with their parents.

There is a footnote to my story. Just before my daughter's seventh Christmas and hours after a conversation with her about placing limits on her endless requests for gifts, she came into the den with an announcement: "I've decided to believe in Santa again." With a sly little smile, she handed me a new list.

I shared these experiences with my caller, but my reasoning and stories had no positive effect on her. She assured me that her daughter was devastated by the news that the headmaster didn't believe in Santa Claus.

Although she was very angry with me, I fought being defensive. I knew her well and was familiar with some of the issues with which she struggled. A divorced mother of three, she lived on income from her domineering parents. Much in her adult life had gone wrong, but she had very pleasant memories of childhood. The maintenance of a number of myths in her life seemed important for her emotional equilibrium. Her children were growing away from her, and she could see a time when she would be alone. She desperately wanted to keep a strong connection with her youngest daughter.

It was also clear from her comments that her daughter had enjoyed delivering the news that the headmaster said Santa was a myth. With all the cruelty that age can sometimes muster, the daughter had delivered the news with some glee, having called on a higher authority to free herself from her mother. I had unwittingly walked into the struggle between an infantilizing mother and the emerging independence in her preteen daughter, all through one sermon illustration.

This experience underscored for me the most important principle at work in all parent/child relationships. The most pivotal factor in long-term, healthy relationships between children and parents is truth. Adults often misunderstand or simply try to ignore a profound characteristic of the moral makeup of young people: Truth doesn't come in sizes. Adults create comfortable little categories that stretch from white lies to perjury, and we draw a moral line somewhere along the way. Often, during the investigation of President Clinton, our children heard on television that "everyone lies about sex." This kind of casuistry is foreign to children; they have to learn it from us.

From a very early age, children are acutely aware of being laughed at or misled by adults. Even good-natured teasing of children by adults and older siblings can hurt children deeply. When we get young children to repeat something cute they said earlier, so another adult can join in the laughter, children learn that only inside knowledge of what is funny to the adult can save them from being the butt of a joke. All bullies learned that to "laugh at" is better than being "laughed at."

A child learns that to "know" is to have control. A person without knowledge is a person without control, a person subject to the whims and derisive laughter of others. However, the innocence of early childhood is endearing, and we adults often mourn its passing. Some of us even try to manipulate events, to control knowledge, in order to prolong our enjoyment of our children's childhood. God knows about the dangers of this inclination. That is why God preserved the story of how Adam and Eve preferred a bite of fruit from the tree of knowledge to the utopia God had created for them in the garden. This Genesis story beautifully illustrates the high price children are willing to pay for knowledge of the world around them.

"You Will Not Die"

> The woman said to the serpent, "We may eat of the fruit of the trees in the garden; but God said, 'You shall not eat of the fruit of the tree that is in the middle of the garden, nor shall you touch it, or you shall die.' " But the serpent said to the woman, "You will not die." (Gen. 3:2–4)

The scene in the garden of Eden is reminiscent of scenes replayed in every home with a toddler. The mobility of the toddler brings a certain amount of terror into the lives of parents. There are poisons, bone-breaking heights, sharp objects, and places that are dangerously hot. The wise parent is diligent. Use of verbal prohibitions help ensure some additional degree of safety, but curiosity is a much stronger force in a child's mind than any parental caution. Kid's daredevil antics fill most parents with fear. We always underestimate what they can get into, as well as the speed with which they can do it. It is understandable that we parents, anxious to keep our toddlers safe, sometimes exaggerate. We try this tactic again when they become teenagers and settle behind the wheel of a car. Our intention is not dishonesty; we only hope to protect the child. Too often, however, we cavalierly sacrifice the truth and suffer unintended consequences.

I once was in a group of young parents who were seeking a way to rear their children according to the precepts of Christianity. As we went around the room to introduce ourselves, each of us was encouraged to bring up any specific issues of concern. When it came her time, one mother said she had a three-year-old who was asking a lot of questions about God. She felt she needed some help with the answers. Her own attempts didn't seem to be working. For example, the mother tried to tell the child about God. She had carefully explained to the child that God is a force, a presence always with us, all around us. This force loves us and will protect us.

The young mother then decided to check what the child had learned. She asked, "Does that answer your questions about God?" The child said, "Yes, God is a horse!"

Children want the truth about God, not watered-down euphemisms. They want knowledge they can rely upon, and they always resent it when the truth is kept from them. God has shown us what happens when we try to keep children in the dark.

> Out of the ground the Lord God made to grow every tree that is pleasant to the sight and good food, the tree of life also in the midst of the garden, and the tree of the knowledge of good and evil. (Gen. 2:9)

When God instructs Adam and Eve not to eat from the tree of "the knowledge of good and evil," it is a simple command, but one that has disturbing implications. Why keep God's children away from knowledge? In Bill Moyers' PBS series on Genesis, one of his guests, Robin Darling, noted that a high school student once told her of God's command that, "He was trying to keep us in the dark." Darling, a professor of theology, adds, "I think that's absolutely right."[1] It seemed to the student, and even to some scholars, that God in this Genesis story was simply acting like the confused parent, trying in vain to keep children ignorant and childlike forever.

Actually, two trees are referred to in the garden story: the tree of life and the tree of knowledge. Yet only the tree of knowledge is forbidden, and it is this one that attracts Adam and Eve. And why not? If Adam and Eve are childlike, then they, like all children, probably assume they will live forever. Youth has life in abundance; it is knowledge they want. Children assume immortality from their first breath through young adulthood. I remember talking to a Naval officer who helped train Navy SEALs, the special forces used for extremely dangerous military missions. After seeing some of the rigorous and potentially deadly training in which these young men were engaged, I said, almost to myself, that I could never do that. The commander heard my comment and quickly observed that, "Of course you couldn't, you're too old." At first I misunderstood his point. He quickly clarified his comment by saying, "It's because they are just kids that they will do this stuff; they think they are never going to die!"

Did God really think that Adam and Eve would choose to be ignorant, naive, and child-like forever? Or is the point of the story to show how foolish we are to try to keep our children naive? For our children to become wise, to know the difference between good and evil, should be the wish of every parent. Yet a profound undercurrent of grief comes over us as we see them grow and become more worldly wise. Perhaps that grief tempts us to want to keep them childlike a little while longer. Of course, we don't want our children to be naive all their lives. Think how vulnerable they would be if they were kept in a pure childlike state all their days.

During a Bible lesson at home with my daughter at age eleven, she read aloud from the King James version the passage in Matthew 25 where Jesus teaches about the wise and foolish virgins. As soon as she read the word, "virgins," she looked up from the text, our eyes met, and I detected embarrassment. She quickly looked down, continuing to read. I knew her glance was to measure my reaction to the word "virgin," curious about what I would say, fearful that I would embarrass her. Thus the game began; the game was about information about sex. It is a game that must be played by all adults with emerging adolescents. I knew it was my move. Finally, after we had discussed the meaning of the passage, I found the courage to say: "By the way, do you know what a virgin is?"

"Ah huh," she grunted in "pre-teenese." Using a technique familiar to all teachers, I matter-of-factly answered my own question to ensure the student heard the answer I wished. "Yes, the girls in this story are young girls who aren't married and who haven't yet had sex. They were considered very special in the Bible. In this story, they have the responsibility of meeting the bridegroom and ushering him and his fellows into the right place for the wedding service to make sure they don't stumble upon the bride before the wedding."

Our eyes met. This time there was no embarrassment. I had acknowledged sex and the role of the virgin in the story, and had set the stage for further honest exchanges on the delicate subject of sex. But, frankly, it took a toll on me. I was sorry that my daughter, at such a young age, knew what a virgin was and knew the word "sex" existed. It made me sad to think she was gaining this knowledge. Yet, conversely, I was glad she was learning about these matters at school and from her parents and, most importantly, that I could speak openly with her about them. At one level, we would all like to keep from our children the scary parts of the world, while, at another less selfish and healthier level, we must acknowledge that it is better for them to learn from us how wondrous sex and love can be. Adults travel most of the road through parenthood conflicted. We want our children to be popular, but not too popular; to get telephone calls from friends, but not too many; and later to be asked out, but, of course, not too often.

Snakes

One part of the Genesis story should serve as a warning to all parents. One can read textual glosses that suggest God was not really talking about literal, instantaneous death when God threatened, ". . . or you shall die" (Gen. 3:3). Some believe God's words simply signaled the introduction of mortality into the human experience. I suspect that Adam and Eve probably thought of dying in its normal meaning: the immediate cessation of life.

That is what makes their choice to cross God and chance death all the more terrifying. The important message here for parents is that had God not added, ". . . or you shall die," the serpent would have had no weapon to use against God's children. The serpent knew that the "parent" had kept the truth from Adam and Eve. He knew that they would not die, at least not instantaneously, if they ate the fruit. Through this story, God shows us the power we give to the serpents of our children's world when we are not the purveyors of the whole truth. If parents are not reliable truth tellers to the young, then we shouldn't be surprised when our children later seek out others for answers to questions of great importance.

As God does in all the parenting roles described in Scripture, God takes this position to show us the consequences of our actions as parents. The serpent does not coerce Adam and Eve, he just adds, "God knows that when you eat of it your eyes will be opened, and you will be like God" (Gen. 3:5). The serpent knows the truth, knows what the children want to know, and knows that the parent has not told the children the whole truth. The serpent needs no additional weapon. He wields the most powerful weapon of all: truth.

By the end of the story, the relationship of trust that had existed between God and God's children in the garden of Eden has been altered. After the encounter with the snake, the very next thing Adam and Eve choose to do is hide from God. Adam says he hides because ". . . I was afraid . . ." (Gen. 3:10). Fear enters a child's life when adults are not reliable. Genesis shows that the shattering of the trust relationship leaves Adam and Eve on their own, brings pain into their lives, and forever alters the relationship between God and all that God has created.

The message to parents from the garden story is simple in concept, but very hard to practice: Knowledge is at the heart of trust. If we don't lie to our children, they will learn to trust us. If we don't lie to them, perhaps they won't lie to us or to themselves. However, to choose to be a truth-teller to our children requires that we believe deeply in the power of truth. The serpent doesn't threaten Adam and Eve, nor does he promise them anything he cannot deliver. He gains his authority in their lives by putting the Word of God in doubt.

Truth and Consequences

The punishment of Adam and Eve is a kind of death, perhaps more terrible than they initially feared. It must have grieved God's heart to punish those whom God loved, but the gift of freedom given to Adam and Eve brought a price for both Creator and created. I often hear from parents that they couldn't sustain the punishment with which they had threatened their child because the punishment ended up punishing the parents too much. "No television for a month!" can often be as hard on the parent as it is on the child. "You can't drive again until you are 25!" is known to the child as toothless hyperbole. Children need punishments that are well reasoned. Allowing the angry reaction to disobedience to shape our punishments is unfair to the child and ultimately to us. One parent's unilaterally imposing a punishment on a child can also strain a marriage.

Parents should remember that the best punishment of a child is administered swiftly and dispassionately. All good punishment is related in some way to the transgression, and the reasoning behind the punishment should always be explained to the child. Punishment should be brief and designed to inconvenience the child, not the whole household. Most of all, productive punishment of children is administered in such a way that the parent's love for the child is never brought into question. Finally, the punishment of a child should always be based on consistent principles of parenting, not on power.

Keep in mind, neither rules for behavior nor the punishment for disobedience should get too complicated. Remember, God gave Adam and Eve only one rule in the garden, and they broke that. God gave Moses only Ten Commandments and we seem unable to keep them. We shouldn't expect much better from children. Besides, even the most diligent parent can't make rules to cover every possibility. A very experienced schoolmaster once told me not to make too many rules about student behavior. He spoke from experience; he once had a request from a frustrated faculty member who wanted to make a rule that students couldn't put peas up their noses in the dining room!

We must never forget that children learn the most important lessons in life from their parents. They learn some of the bad ones, too. I was dumbfounded one time when a high school boy lied to two teachers about a very insignificant matter. He lied to avoid having some minor privileges curtailed. His lies about the matter made things much worse. Yet, he clung to his lies despite appeals from friends and adults to tell the truth and avoid conflict with the school's Honor Code. For some unexplained reason, the boy pressed on. Eventually, I received a recommendation to dismiss him from school by a very frustrated student Honor Council, which found him guilty of a conscious premeditated breach of the Honor Code. Two days after the dismissal, we received a call from the boy's father asking the school to falsify the reason for the dismissal if the boy's new school called us. An apple doesn't fall far from the tree!

In contrast, I have met some extraordinary parents who teach their children lessons about honesty that they can draw on for the rest of their lives. These are parents who aren't afraid of the truth, and, like Abraham, they trust God to take their commitment to the truth and their love for their children and to bring good things into the lives of their children because of it.

One man, a police officer, taught his son a great deal about trusting the truth and God. One morning when I arrived at school, my secretary told me this man was waiting for me. When he entered my office, I could tell something was very wrong. He began his story, visibly shaking, with an apology to me and a reassurance that if what he told me resulted in his son's dismissal, "It will only deepen my respect for you and this school." With those words, he began telling a story about events that took place the night before.

He had been pressing his son to work harder in school. The boy was not doing much homework, not applying himself as the father thought he should. The boy was a particularly immature ninth-grader and had not developed very serious work habits in the school years before. In response to the father's constant pestering, the boy was beginning to show some signs of greater effort. The evening before our meeting, the boy had showed his father a history assignment that his teacher had allowed him to take home to complete. "Will this be graded?" asked the father. "Yes, and look, I've done more than she even asked," the boy said, proudly displaying his work.

After dinner the father was doing the dishes when the phone rang. He overheard his son talking to his history teacher. The teacher was calling because as she was grading the tests from the day, she discovered she didn't have the boy's paper and she wondered if he had turned it in. The boy assured her that the paper in question had been turned in.

"Who was that?" the father asked after the boy had hung up the phone.

"My history teacher. She lost my paper."

"What paper?"

"Oh, we had a test the other day, and a lot of kids did poorly. The teacher said that she thought we knew more about the material than the test showed, so she challenged us to make up our own questions about the chapter and to answer them as a way of showing what we really know. Some of us didn't finish during class, so she gave us extra time in the library," answered the boy.

"That sure was nice of her."

"Yeah, but she lost my paper."

The father said that his son's response troubled him the rest of the evening. Teachers don't often lose papers. He feared that his son was lying. The father sat up much of the night worrying.

"At 2:00 A.M., I couldn't take it anymore," he told me. "So, I got him out of bed and asked him if he had lied to his teacher." The boy denied it.

"It was here that my training as a detective kicked in," he said. "Something didn't smell right. The teacher asked him to make up questions and to answer them," the father recounted his reasoning to me, "but my son showed me a list of questions he says he had done as extra work. But his questions didn't have answers. Then the teacher calls the house asking for the questions and answers she had assigned. I was worried he lied to her, that he never did the whole assignment and faked turning it in. It just didn't make sense."

He told me that he continued questioning his son. He said, "I played good cop, then bad cop. At one point, I told him that I would understand if he hadn't done the assignment. At another point, I asked him to swear on his mother that he was telling me the truth." At 5:00 A.M., "he cracked!" The boy confessed to his father that he had lied. He prepared the questions the teacher asked for but never wrote the answers. "I went to the library like I said, but I never tried the answers," the boy unburdened. "I showed you the questions I had written so you would think I was working harder."

"I'm ashamed of him, but I love him." The father's eyes moistened as he spoke. "Before I came in here, I marched him into his teacher this morning and had him tell her the truth. He is a good boy, but he is willing to be a liar rather than work hard. I will not tolerate that and I know the school wouldn't either. I am sorry my son lied to his teacher and I am sorry he broke the Honor Code." He then reiterated that if I had to dismiss his son, he would understand. After that, he fell silent.

This father taught his son a wonderful lesson that day. He honored the truth even when it wasn't convenient. He also saved his son's place in school. What the father didn't know is that when a student confesses to a violation of the Honor Code before a formal inquiry is undertaken into a possible violation, the student is allowed to stay in school on probation. Because the father had "marched" the boy into the teacher's classroom early in the morning, the lie was corrected before the teacher formally raised the question with the Honor Council. The father's act of trusting the truth had unpredicted benefits; the truth was turned into a positive lesson and a minimal punishment for his son. This father trusted the truth. In so doing, he showed his son the absolute horizon for making moral judgments. I feel certain that someday his son will appreciate what a precious gift he received that day from his father.

Ten Things Parents Can Do to Teach Truth

1. Decide to believe in the truth.

2. Believe in your child: The truth makes children stronger.

3. Allow children to attend a funeral, and let them see you grieve. That is how they learn to grieve in a healthy way.

4. To gauge what to tell children, ask them what they want to know.

5. Remember, the communication parents seek with their teenagers is lost not in the great mysteries of puberty, but in the small lies they told their children earlier in life.

6. When believing in childhood myths like Santa Claus and the Tooth Fairy don't make sense to a child any longer, stop pretending they are real.

7. Remember, if you aren't a truth-teller to your child, you are giving others power over your children.

8. Punishment of a child should be swift, related to the crime or misdeed, and delivered dispassionately by a loving parent.

9. Keep the rules for children easy to understand and few in number. Remember, God gave us only ten commandments. Why should our children have more?

10. Teaching children to believe in the truth as young people gives them an absolute moral horizon against which they can make their own moral decisions.

Chapter 5

The Freedom to Doubt

> I don't have the kind of blind faith Abraham had. I don't
> believe that if a knife is held to my child's throat, an angel
> will come down from heaven to save him. If I don't have
> Abraham's faith, how can I encourage my child to have faith?
> When I have profound questions, how can I encourage my
> child to believe?

I think it would be refreshing to most clergy if people were that honest! However, instead of confronting these questions, many people in church pews often just accept a kind of double life. One life is lived in the everyday world, and the other is reserved for the beliefs they profess on Sunday mornings. These worlds often remain unreconciled. Parents, however, usually don't have that luxury. Because parents frequently get questions about belief from their children, they can't just fake it. It seems, however, that parents often have a very difficult time talking about faith. Many students have told me that their parents never talk to them about anything related to religion. Their parents seem to feel more uncomfortable talking with their children about spiritual issues than they do about sex.

Adults avoid spiritual questions because they sense how enormously complicated the subject is, and they don't feel confident that they know much about it. Unfortunately, young people who do not learn about spiritual issues at home may never be exposed to them in our modern world. Sex education is required in most schools, yet religion is not welcome in many. Sunday school curriculum is rarely systematic and is always voluntary. Unfortunately, many Sunday school teachers aren't trained very well. Consequently, most Christians grow up with a haphazard sprinkling of information about matters of faith and religion. No wonder the church seems irrelevant to them. Worse still, young people become vulnerable to those who offer them easy answers to difficult spiritual questions.

A friend once observed that the success of television evangelists lies in their ability to remove doubt. By substituting certainty for truth, they dispel the doubts of their audiences. An individual does not need to follow the rantings of televangelists to expect certainty from religious leaders. Clergy know that congregations expect them to have resolved all questions of doubt before they enter the pulpit. Many Christians want a shot of certainty on Sunday mornings that will keep them immune to the virus of doubt all week long. I learned this early from my Uncle Bob.

Uncle Bob

One evening when I was a senior in seminary, I spoke with my uncle by phone. He was upset. He was an archetypical Presbyterian layman: conservative, hardworking, successful, self-made, and serious about his church. He was a respected member of the business community of his town. As a member of the Rotary Club and the country club who rarely missed church, it was natural to assume that, at some point, he would be asked to serve on the session, the ruling body of the local Presbyterian Church he attended.

When the call came, my uncle had met with the pastor to discuss the duties of being an elder of the church. From his tone on the telephone, I could tell that the conversation with the minister had not gone well. In fact, early in the conversation he told me that he had been deeply troubled by what the minister had said, and he wanted to know what I thought.

At their meeting, the minister began by asking my uncle if he had any questions. Bob didn't have any questions about the responsibilities he was being asked to take on; rather, he had a doubt. It wasn't that Bob didn't believe in God; he just didn't believe that he had a faith sufficient to speak to others about commitment to the church. Bob knew he would be asking people to support the church, a responsibility he readily accepted because he himself was generous. However, to my uncle Bob, leadership of the church required more than generosity or fiduciary wisdom. To be selected an elder was to be chosen to be an example to others; to Bob that meant one had to have an unshakable faith. Bob confessed to the minister that he had doubts about some issues of faith and for that reason should probably wait a while before becoming an elder.

It was then that the minister shocked him. Mistakenly sensing a kindred spirit, the minister told my uncle that he had doubts, too. In fact, he was presently going through something of a crisis of faith and having serious doubts about what he believed.

Bob didn't like what he heard. My uncle felt it was unconscionable for a minister who leads worship each Sunday, preaching the gospel, to secretly harbor doubts. As a layman, he felt that he could sit in the pew and worship with his doubts, but he was disappointed and angry that a man whose doubts might be even more pivotal than his own was preaching to him. The clergyman's surreptitious doubts sounded hypocritical to Bob.

It seemed incomprehensible to Uncle Bob that someone who was struggling with his own faith could help someone else. Parents can feel that way too. Parents may abdicate their responsibility to nurture faith in their children because they have doubts and questions. In talking with parents about this matter, I have come to understand their predicament. Many spent their formative years attending schools where religious faith was scorned, where they were taught that all faith led to superstition and all religion to prejudice. They emerged from their college days convinced of the hypocrisy of the church and the futility of religious reflection. Now, in adulthood and with the responsibility of parenthood upon them, they have nothing to say to their children about God.

To explore religious belief requires a willingness to ask some fundamental questions about the nature of the world, the purpose of life, and the existence of God. These are big questions, and consideration of them is hard work. To reconsider what we believe or don't believe means facing the fact that what we were taught in school might not have been the liberating vision of life we thought. Instead of being freed from the shackles of religious prejudice, we were taught a simple-minded, godless view of the world—one that cannot sustain the human spirit.

Matters of faith are not easily ignored or kept on an emotional shelf forever. Sometimes tragedy changes that, but many times it is the arrival of a child that raises new fundamental questions about faith in God. Young children are very spiritual creatures. They often sense the presence of God in life. Naturally, they turn to their parents with questions.

St. Paul aptly uses an athletic metaphor[1] when he describes the practice of faith. Spiritual growth and religious reflection, like athletic skills, require training. Bodies without exercise, and skills never tried or only developed in some elementary way, will not support rigorous adult-level play. Many parents don't feel very well coached or in very good spiritual shape to address their children's questions.

Unfortunately, churches often do not direct a sufficiently compelling ministry to parents and children who have been set spiritually adrift.

As the church at Laodicea was condemned by John for its "lukewarm" religion (Rev. 3:14ff.), I fear that mainline churches that are not responding to the needs of families will deserve no better. To meet the demand for quick and easy engagement with religion, especially for "unchurched" generations, easy-answer evangelical fundamentalism has arisen in many places. Within Catholic and traditional mainstream Protestant churches, evangelical fundamentalism has increased its presence particularly amongst the religiously naive. In a culture of "sound bites," quick answers to difficult questions have replaced the historic pedagogy of the Christian church, which rested upon thoughtful reflection, quiet prayer, and serious study.

Those who peddle what I have described as doubtless evangelical fundamentalists know this well. They also know that children are the most susceptible to their message. Our children are proselytized by Christian youth organizations with pre-packaged answers to all of life's questions. These campus crusaders encourage our children to quickly embrace certainty instead of struggling to understand God's truth.

If not in the clutches of the doubtless evangelical fundamentalist, our children remain in the hands of an even more powerful force in our society. In our schools, a cynical, godless postmodernism is the steady drumbeat heard in most classrooms. Vaclav Havel puts the matter in perspective with this very wise observation:

> Today, this state of mind, or of the human world, is called post-modernism. For me, a symbol of that state is a Bedouin mounted on a camel and clad in traditional robes under which he is wearing jeans, with a transistor radio in his hands and an ad for Coca-Cola on the camel's back. . . . The world of our experiences seems chaotic, confusing. Experts can explain anything in the objective world to us, yet we understand our own lives less and less. We live in the post-modern world, where everything is possible and almost nothing is certain.[2]

One spring evening I turned to the local television news and saw a report on a group of third graders who had visited a junior college at the invitation of a professor of philosophy. This was a visit designed to demythologize her dying academic discipline. The reporter dutifully asked the young visitors what questions they had about philosophy and what they had learned from their visit. I was impressed that the children weren't the least bit shy of the microphone, nor were they taken aback by the questions. Each child interviewed had enjoyed the visit. When the reporter inquired about what questions they had asked the professor, they mentioned third-grade versions of "What is the meaning of life?"

What really caught my attention was what the professor said when she spoke with the reporter. Far less comfortable with the microphone than her young visitors, she pronounced the day a great success. She stated she loved talking to this age group because, "They are not afraid to ask questions that have no answers."

The professor did not understand that the classic function of philosophy is to seek exactly the kind of truth these children sought. With her statements, she revealed the mind-set of which Havel spoke. The postmodern secularist believes that there are no answers to the great questions of life and all assertions outside of science are just opinions. Therefore, truth and its implications for human behavior, what we call morality, are all a matter of opinion.

This perspective has affected the mainstream churches as well. Jack Rogers traces the decline in mainstream Protestant church membership[3] to the same unresolved conflicts Havel sees in the world:

> In the 1990's our world view conflicts are increasingly couched in terms of our individual experience. . . . When that happens the experience of one's individual. . . experience becomes ultimate. Then meaningful conversation with those who do not share in that individual experience becomes difficult, if not impossible.[4]

In his book *The Closing of the American Mind*, Allan Bloom saw this same problem in the classroom.[5] Students of all ages come to issues of art, literature, history, and culture with the unshakable assumption that their opinions, no matter how poorly informed, are as good as those opinions held by any teacher, parent, or scholar. This conviction, Bloom contends, is held regardless of the strength of the argument against their position and can only be shaken by the presentation of "scientific facts." Science is invoked as the last word because our children have been taught that science is truth.[6]

Curiously, legitimate science never makes claims of providing truth. All good science restricts itself to the quest for verifiable data and the development of reliable theory. Only pseudo-science makes sweeping statements based on tentative data. Stephen L. Carter, an Episcopalian and a professor of law at Yale, in his excellent book, *The Culture of Disbelief: How American Law and Politics Trivialize Religious Devotion*, sees a dangerous stifling of thoughtful exchange of ideas between mainstream Christians and the dominate secular culture:

[M]embers of religious traditions that teach their followers "truths" about the world are suspect in the liberal world view when they speak those truths in the public square. After all, the public square relies on dialogue as the tool for discovering truth, and individuals who will dismiss as deceptive all evidence against their view can hardly be viewed as welcoming dialogue.[7]

Faith Is Not the Opposite of Doubt

Parents today have a difficult task. Parents and their children can be lured to what appear to be opposite extremes by either a simple-minded evangelical fundamentalism or godless postmodern pseudoscientific secularism. Often, the mainstream church's message is not clearly presented as a viable option to those parents who do not regularly attend church. The traditional church's message is frequently characterized as shallow and naive by the dominant secular culture or as ponderous and insincere by the fundamentalist right. Many modern parents feel that they are not equipped to provide themselves or their children with a spiritual anchor when pummeled by such powerful winds.

If we had a better understanding of Christian doubt, this would not be the case. We need not be torn between the absolutist view of Uncle Bob or the philosophy professor's disdain for questions of ultimate meaning. The church has a sound and compelling message, which is based on Scripture. However, a child's ability to receive and understand this message first requires the adults rearing her and teaching her to appreciate that religious doubts are not a weakness, but a natural and important part of a Christian's faith journey. To achieve this understanding requires a careful look at the precarious premises upon which these extremist messages are founded. The hidden similarities in the messages of both evangelical fundamentalism and secularism must also be considered. To gain the necessary insight needed to refute fundamentalism and postmodern secularism, we must briefly paddle up some intellectual and cultural tributaries and explore the historical influences that come together to form the new mainstream in American culture.

The battle over what American children will believe is being fought in our public schools. In its infancy, several mainstream Protestant denominations supported the creation of a public school system. It was thought that Catholic children could attend parochial schools. Protestant children would attend schools free of sectarian doctrine where children from all Protestant denominations could come, read the Bible, and pray together.

The academic curriculum would reflect the best scholarship and teaching methods. That was the idea, but it hasn't worked out that way.

What the founders of the American public system didn't foresee is that learning can never be completely divorced from belief. But, belief need not fetter open inquiry. In fact, it can be argued that the Christian faith encouraged the very scholarship that has ended up challenging it on several fronts. Although the trial of Galileo may be a dark moment in the history of the church, it is, for the most part, the exception in the church's long history. The church has long supported schools and institutions of higher learning. Especially in this country, many of our finest colleges and universities, as well as medical schools, have been founded by Protestant denominations and the Catholic Church. At their root, scholarship and Christian faith have the same goal. To know more about God's world is to know more about God.

The biblical God, however, has become unwelcome in the public schools. It wasn't scholarship that pushed God out but a new religion. The reaction to this new religion has resulted in a dangerous backlash in Protestant Christianity. The new radical evangelical fundamentalism that tolerates no doubts by its believers, together with its political arm, the Christian Coalition, have declared a cultural war on the godless religion of the public schools. Our children are caught in the middle of this fight in which the God of the Bible and the theology of mainstream Christianity are being squeezed out. Anyone who cares about American public education, anyone who has a child who will be caught in the crossfire of this cultural war, must know what is at stake, how we got to this point, and how we can help our children.

America's Religion

John Dewey, in the early twentieth century, forged the idea of a public school system without God. He based his ideas on the work of a man he greatly respected, William James.[8] James, an early-nineteenth-century philosopher, is best known for his book *The Varieties of Religious Experience*. As important as that work was in describing the nature of belief, his less-known contributions to a new kind of philosophy known as American Pragmatism have had a more profound influence on American education. James was bold enough to call his ideas a "religion,"[9] a new religion that encompassed the best of all the religions, as well as the best science had to offer. His new religion was godless. Dewey believed, with James, that all religion was mostly unproven myth.

James thought the unique environment of America required a new religion. James's uniquely American religion incorporated two of the most widely held American ideals: faith in pragmatic reason and faith in the glorious future that scientific discoveries would bring. He immodestly wrote of his ideas:

> The type of pluralistic and moralistic religion that I have offered is as good a religious synthesis as you are likely to find. Between the two extremes of crude naturalism on one hand and transcendental absolutism on the other, you may find that what I take the liberty of calling the pragmatistic and melioristic type of theism is exactly what you require.[10]

The word *melioristic* is important here and gives us the key to the religion that would eventually take over all public education. Meliorism is the belief that society is always getting better. In contrast to this view of the world, the Judeo-Christian traditions teach that ours is a fallen world. Humans, in the biblical tradition, are corrupt. Adam chose disobedience rather than obedience to God, and we have inherited his sin. Without the grace of God, humankind cannot be saved nor the world reconciled with God. James's pragmatism held that human beings are good and that, with all discoveries, society moves forward toward further improvement. We are the masters of the universe. James's ideas have greatly influenced our current attitude toward public policies: We think that if we make the right laws, society will move forward. His work resonated with the emerging "can-do" spirit of American industrialism in the late nineteenth and early twentieth centuries.

Dewey's ideas about schools and James's ideas about his new religion were built on older ideas that came out of Europe during the seventeenth century. The Enlightenment, with its burst of art, science, and philosophy, had powerful devotees in America. Perhaps the most prominent was the Sage of Monticello, Thomas Jefferson. In a sense, Jefferson was the first American Pragmatist. Although he fathered the Virginia Act of Religious Freedom and was a nominal Episcopalian, Jefferson believed that reason and education, not religion, would ultimately free the human spirit from the prejudices of the past. He wrote to a friend in 1816:

> Enlighten the people generally, and tyranny and oppressions of the body and mind will vanish like evil spirits at the dawn of day. . . I believe [the human condition] susceptible of much improvement and, most of all, in matters of government and religion; and that the diffusion of knowledge among the people is to be the instrument by which [it] is to be effected.[11]

The intoxicating scientific discoveries and advancements in technology of the seventeenth, eighteenth, and nineteenth centuries fueled enthusiasm for a philosophical tradition freed from ancient prejudices, ecclesiastical oppression, and dependency on what was considered superstition. Science and the prospect that in time people might control the internal and external forces that limited their lives were thought to be the new savior. Salvation and happiness were not in the hands of an immutable god; our destiny was in our own hands.

Jefferson had none of the radical intentions for education of William James or James's future disciple, John Dewey. Jefferson fully embraced the idea that education would free men from the "tyranny and oppressions of the body and mind," but he always acknowledged the role of conventional systems of belief. He understood, as sociologist Peter L. Berger wrote, that "morality of Western Civilization has its roots in Christianity and farther back in Judaism."[12]

In fact, few of the supporters of the Enlightenment ever intended to abandon the entire religious heritage of western civilization. Historian Robert Nesbit noted that the politics of power had a great deal to do with the initial Enlightenment attack on religious authority:

> The Renaissance humanists detested much of the ecclesiastical structure of Christianity in their day, but they were profoundly concerned with Christian creed. True atheists were few and far between in the Enlightenment.[13]

Dewey, in contrast, found all religion oppressive and an obstacle to learning. In the prestigious Gifford Lectures of 1929, Dewey systematically laid out his theory of scientific humanism in which human action is linked to objective knowledge. He dismissed what he called the "internal division"[14] in philosophy, which tried to incorporate the great advances of science into antiquated religious principles. With the Hebrew and Christian philosophical description of the natural world as "fallen," the contemporary problem of trying to square new scientific discoveries with an old philosophical mind-set created an intellectually unsustainable dualism. Essentially, the modern "believer," no matter the religious tradition, had to turn off his brain in order to worship. As we noted earlier, Dewey's analysis describes the predicament many people feel they are in today.

Dewey's system called for the replacing of old mythical premises about good and evil. His schools would be free of preconceived notions about the world. Science would bring us facts, and human action would be based on empirical data, not ancient mythologies. The purveyors of these myths and prejudice, the church and parents, would have to be stripped of their power. A new educational system would have to be created that embodied Dewey's ideas; today, we call his creation public schools.

Dewey's ideas attracted tremendous support from those anxious to break society free from the shackles of the past. Stephen Carter reminds us of the powerful disciples Dewey's ideas attracted:

> In *Wisconsin v. Yoder*, Justice William O. Douglas disagreed with the majority's decision to allow the Old Order Amish to remove their children from school. . . . Thus, Douglas argued, "It is the student's judgment, not his parents', that is essential."[15]

The American public schools still remain the most enduring monument to the philosophy of James and Dewey. In 1982, a clarion call was made for the reform of our public schools in *A Nation at Risk*.[16] Despite the general concern in our country that American public schools are not adequately educating our children, and despite the national and statewide efforts to substantively change the public schools, they have not fundamentally changed.

It is not the academic failings of Dewian schools alone that has troubled Americans. Many worry about the moral lessons children are not learning. The ideas of James and Dewey came from the Enlightenment, and the greatest expression of Enlightenment ideas on moral education came from the French philosopher Rousseau. It is through Rousseau's influential work *Emile* that we get our clearest look at the roots that eventually grew into Dewey's educational philosophy. The philosopher writes, "Reason alone teaches us to know good and bad."[17]

Allan Bloom, in the introduction to his translation of *Emile*, writes of Rousseau's new child, "Nothing will be accepted on authority; the evidence of his senses and the call of his desires will be his [the child's] authorities."[18] Bloom continues:

> [O]nly clear and distinct evidence should ever command belief. . . all his knowledge should be relevant to his real needs. . . . In a sense, Rousseau makes his young Emile an embodiment of the Enlightenments's new scientific method.[19]

Rousseau, James, and Dewey have had their way with American education, but things may be changing.

> A massive intellectual revolution is taking place that is perhaps as great as that which marked off the modern world from the Middle Ages. The

foundations of the modern world are collapsing. . . The principles forged during the Enlightenment (c. 1600–1780), which formed the foundations of the modern mentality, are crumbling.[20]

With these dramatic words, Professor Diogenes Allen, of Princeton Theological Seminary, begins an analysis of the current intellectual revolution. The disintegration of what Allen calls the "four pillars" of the Enlightenment will have a profound effect on the future. These pillars form the support structure upon which public education rests. These ideas are that (1) everything that can be known will be found out by scientific investigation; (2) that like the orderly world around us, our inner world——our minds and emotions—are orderly too; (3) that society is "melioristic," and one generation will have it better than the next; (4) and, finally, that all knowledge is good.

Americans don't accept that these pillars are necessarily true anymore. The introduction of the "misery index" in American politics during the '80s marked a change in our thinking. The misery index took into consideration skyrocketing inflation, double-digit interest rates, and record joblessness; it was the formula for measuring the decline of our society. Ronald Reagan's question was answered by the American electorate with an emphatic, "No, we are not better off today than we were four years ago." Previously, the proposition that one generation would not be more prosperous and healthier than the previous was absurd.

Americans are having second thoughts about the benefits of scientific knowledge, as well. I know of a scholar who, while lecturing on eating disorders in young women, worried that her work may have given inadvertent guidance to troubled girls. She feared that by revealing the methods and actions of this self-destructive behavior, others may have been tempted to experiment. For serious scientists, it is a radical departure from the Enlightenment assumptions to wonder if we will be better off knowing less. Congress's quick passage of legislation banning federal funding for human cloning reflects society's new attitude about science: We want the science genie kept in the bottle.

The crumbling of the philosophical underpinnings of our modern world has had a tremendous impact on public education. Dissatisfaction with "godless" public schools, moral relativism, and the persistent general perception that without God morality declines, have all combined to contribute to the rise of evangelical fundamentalism in American Christianity. Beginning in the 1970s with the Moral Majority, this conservative backlash has shown itself most clearly in the political movements it has spawned. Today's embodiment is the Christian Coalition. These groups have had a powerful influence on American public policy as well as on the church. Part of their success has been in identifying a common enemy. Peter L. Berger, an astute observer of the American culture, captured the sense of the Christian Right when he wrote: "It is safe to ascribe to the Enlightenment the origins of a process of debunking every sort of certitude that has led to the moral relativism of our present moment."[21] In Rousseau, James, and Dewey, and the public policies and educational bureaucracies they spawned, the Christian Right have the villains they need.

Now the battle lines in America's culture war[22] have been drawn. On one side are the godless public schools and their hostile attitude toward religion, and on the other side is the Christian Right and its call for America to return to the days of a God-based society. Many of us feel caught in the middle of this war, not wanting schools dominated by either religious doctrine or liberal social policies. We are repulsed by the sanctimonious and regressive attitudes of the Christian Right, and we are worried about the poor state of our schools after decades of Dewey's influence.

If you don't like either extreme, it may be because they have more in common than they first appear. This was first pointed out in a massive study about the world of religious fundamentalism. Buried in the four-volume study sponsored by The American Academy of Arts and Sciences is this sentence:

> "[F]undamentalism is a peculiarly modern brand of religion that shares the ideals. . . of liberalism."[23] (from *Fundamentalism Project*)

Could both extremes of the culture war be cut from the same cloth? You bet! The common characteristics of each are worth considering. They are as follows:

1. An enclave mentality
2. Language control
3. Fostered dependence

Emmanuel Sivan, one of the most insightful contributors to the *Fundamentalism Project*, describes the essential nature of the "The Enclave Culture." He characterized this "inside-outside" orientation as relations between the enclave and what exists beyond its boundary. A. C. Gaebelien, a leading fundamentalist of his day, described the central tenet of his radical fundamentalism in 1914 as "God's greatest call is separation."[24] Being separate from the world is a high priority for all fundamentalism: "[T]he enclave must place the oppressive and morally defiled outside society in sharp contrast to the community of virtuous insiders."[25] A wall of "virtue" (specifically accepted behavior and language) is constructed to separate the "saved" from the lost.

Membership in the enclave is defined through adherence to a subtle combination of feeling separate from and superior to those outside the accepted group. In order to maintain the enclave, it is important to develop a special vocabulary and a set of behaviors that define acceptance. This is where language control comes into play. Whether it's the trademark religious language of the fundamentalist ("Are you born again?") or the politically correct language demanded on university campuses, language control is central to acceptance in the enclave. To deviate from accepted language is to be identified as "outside" and to be targeted for the wrath of the enclave.

Within the membership of the enclave, there is tremendous pressure for compliance. While pretending membership is voluntary, dependency on the group begins to arrest individual growth. The longer one is within the enclave, the harder it is to leave. An enclave always identifies an enemy. Frequently, sweeping generalizations are used to describe those outside the enclave. Phrases like "vast right-wing conspiracy" and "liberal media" are used to paint the enemy. The enclave is portrayed as the only sane response to the enemy's encroachment on its members' freedoms.

Language control is so important to the enclave because language influences thought. This characteristic should especially concern parents and anyone who works with children. From his perspective as a professor at Yale, Stephen Carter sees that different perspectives are not welcome in the collegiate marketplace of ideas. For example, promoting a viewpoint based upon a religious truth, Carter contends, is not credible at liberal universities. Introducing the idea of God as a force in the shaping of historical events is not an acceptable premise for argument in most undergraduate classrooms. It doesn't, however, take sweeping gag orders to create a malevolent atmosphere with subtle restrictions on language. The pervasive political correctness enforced on college campuses can have a profound effect on a culture.[26] Recently, a candidate for a student government office at a major university was demonized by the campus newspaper for his potentially dangerous beliefs. He was a Christian.

Christian Doubt

If both the godless cynicism of liberal educational establishments and the self-righteous Christian Right scare you, there is a middle ground. Mainstream Christianity has a great deal to offer. You see, what Uncle Bob didn't understand, what his minister should have clarified for him, and what I didn't know at the time, is that the Bible teaches us that Christian doubt—thoughtful questions about matters of faith and life—is a healthy part of a life-long spiritual journey. Christians don't have to forbid certain questions or doubt-filled language. The good news is that the doubts Christians have about faith are not weaknesses; rather, they are natural parts of Christians' spiritual journeys. In fact, without a healthy dose of Christian doubt, faith can become stagnant or be reduced to simple zealotry. Our only certainty as a faithful Christian should be God's love for us; we don't have to have all the answers to life's questions.

Self-doubt and Christian doubt, however, are profoundly different. The key difference between the two is that often our personal feelings of doubt are rooted in some event of the past. A crisis of confidence or the fear of failure can lead to self-doubt about our ability to cope with the next situation. A broken heart can lead to fear of new relationships; it can lead to doubts about whether we can ever find love again.

Self-doubt can be paralyzing, but Christian doubt isn't that way. The essential orientation of Christian doubt is toward the future, toward new possibilities in our relationship with God. Christian doubt is not about us, our fears, or our past failures. Rather, Christian doubt is about God and the emerging relationship we have with God.

Christian doubt keeps us engaged with the profound questions of life. It requires us to challenge old assumptions and our tendency toward spiritual complacency. Christian doubt does not undermine our faithfulness; it builds upon it. This idea has always been best expressed by the father of the very ill boy who came to the disciples of Jesus for help. When he didn't get help from the disciples for his son, he didn't lose hope; he turned to Jesus. What Jesus taught him was that the help he was looking for was in the power of faith he already held.

"I Believe; Help My Unbelief!"

Someone from the crowd answered him, "Teacher, I brought you my son; he has a spirit that makes him unable to speak; and whenever it seizes him, it dashes him down; and he foams and grinds his teeth and becomes rigid; and I asked your disciples to cast it out, but they could not do so." He answered them, "You faithless generation, how much longer must I be among you? How much longer must I put up with you? Bring him to me." And they brought the boy to him. When the spirit saw him, immediately it convulsed the boy, and he fell on the ground and rolled about, foaming at the mouth. Jesus asked the father, "How long has this been happening to him?" And he said, "From childhood. It has often cast him into the fire and into the water, to destroy him; but if you are able to do anything, have pity on us and help us." Jesus said to him, "If you are able!—All things can be done for the one who believes." Immediately the father of the child cried out, "I believe; help my unbelief!" (Mark 9:17–24)

What a terrible burden the boy's illness must have been on the entire family. Today epileptic seizures, like the ones described in this passage, are better understood and often controlled by medication. In the first century, however, the terrifying sight of a human being caught in the grip of a grand mal seizure was thought to be connected with demons or secret sins of the father.

Some of the most moving scenes in the New Testament are of desperate people pressing forward through crowds gathered around Jesus to beg for his help. They came to Jesus only after every other possible remedy had been tried. They tried every remedy, of course, but their own faith. This exchange between Jesus and the father is compelling to the modern parent. Although modern medicine could likely control this boy's disease, we still have incurable ailments. However, it is not in the medical details that the meaning of the story resides. Jesus is redirecting the father's search for help to an awesome power. If he exercised his faith, help for the boy's desperate situation was within the father's grasp.

What then are we, as parents, to learn from this father? What do we tell ourselves and our children about faith, especially when doubts linger?

First, we should accept that having doubts is a necessary condition, not an obstacle to Christian growth. It is not something about which we should be ashamed. Christian doubt is the essential catalyst to Christian spiritual growth. Sometimes, spiritual growth is stimulated through sharing doubts with one another. Church groups can be helpful vehicles for adult sharing; but, for the parent, I suggest that conversations with children about faith and doubts are wonderful vehicles for mutual spiritual growth. It was St. Benedict who said, "[T]he Lord often revealeth to the younger what is best."[27] A good venue for these discussions is intergenerational Sunday school classes and study groups, particularly on issues of faith and Christian doctrine. These conversations, if properly constructed, can be a wonderful stimulus for conversation with our children. In these conversations, we don't have to be the authority or the standard bearer. We don't even have to be ahead of the development of our children's faith. We can open lines of communication and enjoy new exchanges with our children. They can help us! Occasionally, replacing "How much homework do you have?"

with "Do you think it matters if we love God?" during a car ride, can result in a conversation that is good for both the parent and the child.

Second, we must teach our children that the Bible gives us a model for how we should approach those areas of Christian doubt that challenge us. As St. Paul might suggest:

Be a Beroean!

After Paul and Silas had passed through Amphipolis and Apollonia, they came to Thessalonica, where there was a synagogue of the Jews. And Paul went in, as was his custom, and on three sabbath days argued with them from the scriptures, explaining and proving that it was necessary for the Messiah to suffer and to rise from the dead, and saying, "This is the Messiah, Jesus whom I am proclaiming to you." Some of them were persuaded and joined Paul and Silas, as did a great many of the devout Greeks and not a few of the leading women. But the Jews became jealous, and with the help of some ruffians in the marketplaces they formed a mob and set the city in an uproar. While they were searching for Paul and Silas to bring them out to the assembly, they attacked Jason's house.

That very night the believers sent Paul and Silas off to Beroea; and when they arrived, they went to the Jewish synagogue. These Jews were more receptive than those in Thessalonica, for they welcomed the message very eagerly *and examined the scriptures every day to see whether these things were so* [my emphasis]. (Acts 17:1–5, 10–11)

The Beroeans are models for all Christians of how to address doubt and other questions of faith. A Beroean bases her faith on the Bible, but is also open to new ideas, unafraid of challenges to old ways of thinking. However, a Beroean is not easily convinced. Even Paul's mighty persuasive powers met with questions from the Beroeans. Notice that they listened politely and were open to Paul's new ideas. Then they went back to the Bible to see if what Paul was saying was a legitimate interpretation of Scripture's message. What an insightful way to approach matters of faith! We could hope for that same attitude for our children as they grow and are exposed to new ideas. The Beroeans knew their God was a big God. They knew that a new idea was not going to ruin their faith or diminish God. Rather, new ideas, even ideas that challenged their current limited understanding of faith, were vehicles for spiritual growth. Doubts raised were an opportunity to grow into deeper faith; they could believe this because their faith was grounded in the Bible.

In the spirit of Beroean Christianity, Ralph C. Wood writes:

> A healthy dose of Christian disbelief or "holy skepticism" would serve
> as a much-needed antidote to the soft-core spirituality that saps much of
> contemporary Christianity, especially in its evangelical expression. . . .
> The church of our time needs a theology that repudiates all saccharine
> substitutes for the hard thinking that the Christian faith requires.[28]

The Beroeans engaged Paul on a common ground and with openness, but
also with a healthy skepticism of new ideas. Paul's idea of a "suffering
Messiah" was new to the Beroeans, and it required them to think about
their faith in a new way. Contrast the responsible reaction and intellectual
openness of the people of Beroea with the fearfulness of the people
of Thessalonica. In Thessalonica, the Greeks were interested in Paul's
ideas, but the Jews were not open to the gospel message. They threw
Paul out of town. Scripture tells us that it wasn't that the people of Thessalonica disagreed with Paul, but they were "jealous"of him. Were they
afraid of the doubts his ideas might raise, jealous of his faith and the
courage it gave him?

Little is known about the town of Beroea during Paul's time. Cicero
describes it as "off the road,"[29] most likely meaning that it was not a center for trade or manufacturing. Evidently Paul was quite successful there,
converting many. The Beroeans put their money where their faith was. We
learn later in Acts 20:4 that "Sopater of Beroea" accompanied Paul to
Jerusalem with his church's share of the collection for the support of the
Church in Jerusalem.

Once the Thessalonians learned of Paul's whereabouts, they followed
him to Beroea; then Paul fled to Athens. There he gave his famous speech
before the intellectuals of Athens in the court of the Areopagus. It was an
honor for Paul to speak at the Areopagus, and he used the occasion to cri-
tique pagan polytheism to the assembled Epicurean and Stoic philosophers.
Paul cleverly ascribed a new meaning to the catch-all altar the Athenians
had erected to the "Unknown God." Paul's speech, recorded in Acts
17:19ff. is theologically important, but more important for parents is the
reaction of the Greek philosophers to the new ideas that Paul raised. When
Paul told the assembled intellectual leaders of Athens that Jesus was not
held by the grave after the crucifixion, but lives, v. 32 reads: *"Some scoffed;
but others said, 'We will hear you again about this.' "* But, they never did.

Like many in our universities today, the intellectuals in Athens only pretended to be open to new ideas. In their own way, these great intellectuals
were just as afraid of Paul's message as were the Thessalonians. Only the

Beroeans listened to Paul, confident that the biblical God they knew was big enough to show them if there was truth in these new ideas.

To stand in the mainstream of American Christianity is to be a Beroean Christian, to be a biblical Christian unafraid of new ideas, but faithful to Scripture as our guide to a life pleasing to God. The Beroeans were not naive, nor did they shut themselves off from the world in a religious enclave. They were intellectually open and fully engaged with the world. In the spirit of Beroea, we read some solid biblical advice:

> Beloved, do not believe every spirit, but test the spirits to see whether they are from God; for many false prophets have gone out into the world. (1 John 4:1)

We rear healthy and faithful children by encouraging them to ask questions about God, by studying Scripture with them, and by being unafraid of new or previously unconsidered ideas. Our God is bigger than all the world's ideas, and if the triumph of the life of Jesus means anything to us, we as his faithful followers need not be afraid of the world.

In the end, we can give our children no better advice than American novelist Flannery O'Connor gave in 1955 to a college freshman who was troubled by the religious doubts that his college professors were raising in his mind. O'Connor wrote: "Even in the life of a Christian, faith rises and falls like the tides of an invisible sea." She continued:

> Learn what you can, but cultivate Christian skepticism. It will keep you free—not free to do anything you please, but free to be formed by something larger than your own intellect or the intellects of those around you.[30]

Ten Things We Can Tell Our Children about Doubt

1. Children should be reassured that their doubts about God are a natural part of growing faith in God.

2. God will not condemn us for doubt. The God of the Bible loves us, doubts and all.

3. Doubts about God are not like self-doubt. Self-doubt has its root in our past; doubts about God have their roots in our future relationship with God.

4. Christian doubt drives us to think and study more about God and to pray.

5. We should question those who say they have all the answers.

6. Faith is like any skill. Without practice, it doesn't improve.

7. Faith leads to lasting truth, and truth sets us free. If it is based on biblical principles, religion won't narrow our vision.

8. Caution your children to be prepared for a bias against ideas that are based on religious conviction. Many schools and colleges are not friendly places for those who believe in God.

9. Tell your child to avoid any group, whether they call themselves Christians or not, that wants them to act in only one way, associate only with approved people, and depend only on the group's leader for authority. The God of the Bible is open to all, regardless of where we start our journey, and only God's authority should rule our lives.

10. Tell your child: Be a Beroean!

Chapter 6

Honor

> Honor your father and your mother, so that your days may be
> long in the land that the LORD your God is giving you.
>
> *(Exod. 20:12)*

After reading this commandment, young people often ask, "Why
doesn't God say anything about how parents are to treat their children?" That the children carry all the burden of this relationship often
seems unfair to high school students. The word *honor* also sounds
oddly anachronistic to them. It's a word they don't hear much in their
world, and it sounds like something only a military school would have
in its motto. Students rarely hear the word *honor* used in most schools
and, when it is used, sincerity is not always linked to it. For example,
children learn that the "Honor Roll" reflects a certain ability to win
grades but does not always reflect sincere scholarship. The golf team
might use it in the sense of "doing the honors, " which simply means
going first. Banks say they will "honor a check," which simply means
they will agree to cash it.

Honor, and its synonym "respect," don't positively resonate with
this generation. I once saw a banner stretched across the entrance area
where high school football players were about to enter the field. The
idea was that the players would rip through the sign as they burst onto
the field to the applause of the fans. The sign was clearly meant to
inspire the underdog to defeat the superior team, who also happened
to be the defending league champions. In an odd way, the words on
the sign seemed to symbolize the attitude of many kids today. It said,
"SHOW NO RESPECT!"

To my young students, the entire biblical relationship between
parent and child seems one-sided, and they don't like it. As one student said of this commandment, "It sure does sound like a father
wrote it." Another student surprised me by noting that the wording

of the commandment made a lot of sense to her, for the commandment would have been impossible to keep if God had said that we must "like" our parents!

However, the Bible is emphatic on this point. If we don't get it in Exodus, two books later in Deuteronomy, the Bible adds a little emphasis:

> "Cursed be anyone who dishonors father or mother." All the people shall say, "Amen!" (Deut. 27:16)

While the commandment is clear, it is challenging to teach children what honoring parents means in a "no respect" culture. We might be tempted to think that the Bible cannot possibly have anything helpful to say to parents and children at the dawn of the twenty-first century. Things have changed too much. In our fast-paced society, the gulf between one generation and the next seems enormous. The difference between Johnny Unitas and Dennis Rodman as sports heroes reflects the abyss in American culture in just two generations.

Are the Ten Commandments of any use to modern parents? Is the commandment to honor our mother and fathers of any use, especially since it seems that it is simply designed to control youth? Is it worth teaching to our youth?

One of the passages that can inform our understanding of the commandment to honor our parents is a passage my students like best. When young people read the story of Jesus in the temple, they wonder:

Did Jesus Honor His Parents?

Jesus was the smothering mother's perfect son, the joke goes. He lived at home until he was thirty, and he never had a job or a girlfriend. He never got married, and his mother thought he was God!

Students like the story of Jesus being left behind in Jerusalem because they more closely identify with Jesus at that point of his life than at any other. The story of the precocious and misunderstood young Jesus who is discovered by his parents learning and teaching in the temple is recorded only in Luke. The story takes place when Jesus is twelve, a young adolescent. Adults might read the story and be struck by the intelligence of this young man; parents and adolescents read it and see a glimpse of struggle familiar to them both:

> The child grew and became strong, filled with wisdom; and the favor of God was upon him. Now every year his parents went to Jerusalem for the

festival of the Passover. And when he was twelve years old, they went up as usual for the festival. When the festival was ended and they started to return, the boy Jesus stayed behind in Jerusalem, but his parents did not know it. Assuming that he was in the group of travelers, they went a day's journey. Then they started to look for him among their relatives and friends. When they did not find him, they returned to Jerusalem to search for him. After three days they found him in the temple, sitting among the teachers, listening to them and asking them questions. And all who heard him were amazed at his understanding and his answers. When his parents saw him they were astonished; and his mother said to him, "Child, why have you treated us like this? Look, your father and I have been searching for you in great anxiety." He said to them, "Why were you searching for me? Did you not know that I must be in my Father's house?" But they did not understand what he said to them. Then he went down with them and came to Nazareth, and was obedient to them. (Luke 2:40–51)

The first characteristic of Jesus that we should notice in this story is his independence. He is well ahead of his years in intelligence and spiritual depth. However, Jesus acts like every other child his age when he shares the common predilection to self-deputize. This age group regularly takes liberties their parents aren't ready to confer.

At first glance, Mary and Joseph may seem irresponsible. They travel an entire day after the festivities in Jerusalem and don't seem to miss their son. However, children of this age cabal together, and it is not unusual for them to run off without a word as soon as they see some friends. It would not surprise me if Mary and Joseph believed that because Jesus had traveled to Jerusalem with friends, he would return to Nazareth with the same group. Maybe he was with his friends at a different part of the throng. At no other time in our adult life do we make more erroneous predictions about human behavior than when we are the parents of a teenager.

What must Mary and Joseph have felt when they looked in vain for Jesus as the families with which they were traveling started to make camp for the night? What panic must have ensued when they realized he was not with the other twelve-year-old boys? What a terrifying nighttime race back to that large, crowded, and dangerous city, hoping to find their son safe and fearing the worst!

While on sabbatical in the south of France one time, my wife, daughter, and I left the small village where we lived for a day trip to Marseilles. The city was seedy and teeming with people. After a tour of the old harbor area, we marched up the hill for a visit to Notre Dame, the magnificent Romanesque church overlooking the city and harbor. We entered the main sanctuary of the church and began looking at the artwork, statuary, and iconography. My daughter, age twelve, said, "I'm going to look around." That fit our routine. We often went our separate ways in churches and museums, each scouting out artwork and curious features. Then we would locate one another and share our findings. After twenty minutes of taking in the many portraits of miraculous rescues at sea, my wife interrupted me.

"Where is she?"

"She said she was going to look around," I said, telling her only what she already knew.

"She's not in here, I'm going to look for her outside," my wife said with no alarm. That seemed like a reasonable idea, because our daughter was fascinated by the gargoyles. Surely, she would be just outside the front door studying the frightening or amusing downspouts that decorated most of these churches. Ten minutes later, my wife found me in front of the Patron Saint of Marseilles. "She's gone!" My wife had searched all around the outside of the church. Nothing. I, of course, panicked as I began to review images in my mind of Gene Hackman being drugged in *The French Connection*, my complete knowledge of Marseilles until our visit that day.

We launched a frantic search. As we burst out the front door of the sanctuary, my daughter bounded up, excited that she had found an observation platform with a spectacular view of the harbor and the Chateau d'If, the dreaded prison that tried to hold the fictional Count of Monte Cristo. The platform's location, of course, made it impossible for my wife to see our daughter during her search of the front of the Church. We sighed with a parent's relief. I forgot about the artwork, but thanked Jesus and the Patron Saint for one more rescue in Marseilles.

Upon reflection, the most interesting aspect of this experience was that neither my wife nor I chastised our daughter for taking the liberty of extending her tour beyond the agreed-upon environs. Only two years earlier, we would have sternly lectured her about the danger of our not knowing her whereabouts. We would have reminded her that Marseilles is a dangerous city full of unspecified people who would do bad things. However, this time we said nothing. We said nothing because we were gradually getting used to her taking small liberties and surviving them. Evidence was mounting that she was able to handle more freedom. My wife and I, on the other hand, were having difficulty handling her freedom. We had no choice but to become accustomed to her growing independence. It's nerve-wracking to be a parent of an adolescent, but her actions were normal. The question remains, "Is she going to be safe when I see her again?" The answer is the same for every parent: maybe.

Any pride Mary and Joseph may have felt when they finally found Jesus safe in the temple with the rabbis was probably postponed. Luke records only a rather subdued reaction on the part of Mary and Joseph. They were "astonished." Frankly, I think after three days of looking for their twelve-year-old son, they were probably a little more than "astonished." They, too, may have been accustomed to his taking liberties. "Child, why have you treated us like this? Look, your father and I have been searching for you in great anxiety." I wonder if Mary screamed those words? Ten minutes in Marseilles ruined my day; three days of searching in Jerusalem would have ruined my life!

The arrival of adolescence awakens a child's innate ability to convey without subtlety one-thousand-and-one ways of telling parents exactly how stupid we are. I think adolescents must get this capacity with their first pimple. Jesus' response to Mary's question is classic teenage-ese: "Why were you searching for me? Did you not know that I must be in my Father's house?"

Luke's marveling at the perspicacity of Jesus doesn't lead him to gloss over one of the facts of rearing an adolescent. Subtly tucked in the text is an important reminder to parents. Even Jesus, after this incident, was put on restrictions for his little stunt. Luke writes that he "went down with them and came to Nazareth and was obedient to them." After this event Jesus was obedient, but his relationship with his mother was not without other testy encounters.

> While he was still speaking to the crowds, his mother and his brothers were standing outside, wanting to speak to him. Someone told him, "Look, your mother and your brothers are standing outside, wanting to speak to you." But to the one who had told him this, Jesus replied, "Who is my mother, and who are my brothers?" And pointing to his disciples, he said, "Here are my mother and my brothers! For whoever does the will of my Father in heaven is my brother and sister and mother." (Matthew 12:46–50)

What did Mary feel upon hearing her son's words? Surely, even the mother of Jesus was not immune to the sting a parent can feel from a child's cruel remark. Mary exhibited a toughness and an emotional resiliency that should be a guide and inspiration to all parents. As a Reformed Christian, I don't pray to Mary, but I very much feel that I have a kindred spirit in her. In many ways, she is a model for modern parents; like many parents, who perhaps thought her job as a parent would be finished when her son was grown, Mary knew there is always something to teach a child, no matter his age.

> On the third day there was a wedding in Cana of Galilee, and the mother of Jesus was there. Jesus and his disciples had also been invited to the wedding. When the wine gave out, the mother of Jesus said to him, "They have no wine." And Jesus said to her, "Woman, what concern is that to you and to me? My hour has not yet come." His mother said to the servants, "Do whatever he tells you." Now standing there were six stone water jars for the Jewish rites of purification, each holding twenty or thirty gallons. Jesus said to them, "Fill the jars with water." And they filled them up to the brim. He said to them, "Now draw some out, and take it to the chief steward." So they took it. When the steward tasted the water that had become wine, and did not know where it came from (though the servants who had drawn the water knew), the steward called the bridegroom and said to him, "Everyone serves the good wine first, and then the inferior wine after the guests have become drunk. But you have kept the good wine until now." Jesus did this, the first of his signs, in Cana of Galilee, and revealed his glory; and his disciples believed in him. After this he went down to Capernaum with his mother, his brothers, and his disciples; and they remained there a few days. (John 2:1–12)

We don't know why Mary felt that Jesus should do something about the awkward situation in which the host found himself. Is it possible that Mary was acutely aware that it was Jesus' wandering entourage that had depleted the wine supply? We can only wonder. The biggest question of all, however, about the miracle at Cana is why Jesus chose to reveal his divinity at such an event. It seems odd that his power to perform miracles was first revealed in order to save a host from embarrassment. Critics of Christianity surely must find some amusement in Jesus' first miracle, but parents should listen carefully to the Gospel message. I think it is for us.

Note Jesus' rather short response to Mary, "Woman, what concern is that to you and to me?" Mary's response is silence, and that speaks volumes. There was no retort, no pleading, no argument or rancor; not even a word. Yet one can almost see the expression that she must have shot at her son before she turned on her heels and instructed the steward to do whatever her son said to do.

In Cana, Mary seemed to force Jesus' public display of his miraculous powers, and then, after a tense exchange and a happy ending to the wedding, Jesus followed Mary home and stayed with her for a few days. Could it be that Mary had something further to tell her son and his followers before he and they would be ready for what lay ahead? Could it be that Mary knew even better than Jesus that the time had come to begin his ministry?

In the Synoptic Gospels,[1] Jesus prepares for his public ministry in the classic holy-man tradition of taking to the desert to be tested and to be purified. In John, Jesus goes to Nazareth with Mary for a few days before he and his disciples begin their work. Did John see this as the last step in Jesus' preparation—not the purifying temptations of the desert, but a heart-to-heart with Mom? Was it in fact his mother who knew even before he the great power he had? After all, she pondered in her heart the strange things that happened in the stable. Did Mary, like most mothers, know more about her son than he did himself? Did she remind him during those days in Nazareth of the boyhood lessons she had taught him? Did she speak again about the faith she had passed on to him?

Some modern biblical scholars have speculated about the influences on Jesus' thinking. Participants in the controversial Jesus Seminar, for example, have wondered if Jesus' teachings may have been shaped by his visits to the Roman city near his home. We can only guess about such matters, but the fact that Jesus' first miracle is compelled by his mother and that he spends his last private moments with her before he begins his public life should be instructive to us. In the rearing of the boy Jesus, I think Mary, and even the mysteriously absent Joseph, must have kept in mind the kind of principles that they hoped he would exemplify when he was a grown man. Perhaps Jesus, like all children, counted his earthly parents the most influential forces in his life. In John's Gospel, Jesus did not go back to the rabbis or into the desert before he began his public ministry; rather, he went home. At least from John's perspective, Jesus may have learned more from Mary than from the rabbis and Romans.

Parents, First Honor Your Parents!

The Bible is not always easy to understand; in fact, some parts are downright confusing. Understanding what the biblical writers' intentions were, let alone ferreting out God's message in Scripture for us, is not always an easy matter.

John Calvin, the great church reformer, understood this problem; about the interpretation of Scripture he conceded that while Scripture is "sufficiently" clear, it is not always "absolutely" clear.[2] In other words, the Bible is not a cookbook or quick answer guide to life's problems, but rather an account of the mighty acts of God. To illuminate one part of Scripture, we must be willing to look at all of Scripture. The Westminster Confession of Faith (1647) gives us a good rule to keep in mind: "The infallible rule of interpretation of Scripture, is the Scripture itself."[3]

Interpreting the Word of God is not, however, a passive academic exercise of comparing one part of Scripture to another. The stakes are much higher than that. Janet Martin Soskice, in *Metaphor and Religious Language*, reminds us that interpreting Scripture is an intensely personal experience. To find God's message for us, we must be open to the possibility of it changing our lives:

> The author's experience is interpreted by his sacred texts, his sacred texts are reinterpreted by his own experience, the whole is founded upon centuries of devotional practice. If there is one insight to be taken from philosophical hermeneutics, it is this—that we interpret texts and they interpret us.[4]

The commandment to honor our parents is one of the most deceptive passages in Scripture. On the surface it seems like a simple command designed to secure family tranquility. However, when we really open ourselves to its meaning, when we look at other passages that shed light on it, we may find that it is not about our children at all; it may be about us. A brief story illustrates my point.

One time, as my wife and I sat in a restaurant with friends, our conversation turned from our children's lives to the new challenges that we faced with aging parents. Each of us felt drawn into our parents' lives in some new way. Some of us at the table carried a new burden of being caretakers of infirmed parents, but even those whose parents were in good health sensed an increasing frailty and dependency in our parents.

One woman shared how she had been recently chastised by her husband for the disparaging way in which she and her siblings burlesqued their increasingly demented mother in their not-so-private telephone conversations. Her husband was concerned that their teenage daughter frequently overheard these conversations that his wife had with her brothers and sisters. She and her siblings were deeply concerned about their mother, and friendly humor eased the worry. Nevertheless, our friend good-naturedly accepted her husband's reproach, acknowledging that someday she might be in her mother's position. She was wise to take her husband's counsel. We can forget sometimes that one of the responsibilities we carry as parents is to teach our children how to treat us. Just as we may never know what our children learned about being a parent until we see how they parent their own children, we may not know what our children learned from us about being a good child until we begin to lose our independence as adults.

A Grimm's fairy tale reminds us of this sad fact. In a tale entitled "The Old Grandfather's Corner," we are told of an old man who lives with his son and daughter-in-law. The old man's hands shake, and he frequently spills soup on the tablecloth and himself. His infirmity annoys his son and daughter-in-law; out of frustration, they ask the grandfather to take his meals in the corner behind a screen so he won't be an embarrassment. He eats his meals from a simple wooden bowl because he had dropped and broken the good one.

One day the father finds his own little boy of four years sitting on the ground trying to assemble some wooden pieces. The father asks, "What are you making?" The boy replies, "I am making a little bowl for papa and mama to eat their food in when I grow up."[5]

Most of us will be dependent on our children in some way later in life. We are commanded by God to honor our parents "so that your days maybe long in the land." Perhaps the most curious aspect of this commandment is that its fulfillment is linked to our future prosperity and longevity. I do not think this is just some echo from a pre–social security agrarian past. It seems the biblical God is telling us that as we grow old and dependent on those around us, the quality of our lives will be more dependent on the relationships we maintain with our families than on the extent of our medical insurance coverage. Perhaps we teach our children honor by showing honor to our parents.

Parents, Honor Your Children!

Many parents today seem confused about how to love their children. That may sound odd, but I think this is at the root of a great deal of confusion children experience regarding how to honor parents. Often we substitute gifts for love. For her insistence on giving trophies (real trophies!) to all first graders on the last day of school to celebrate their accomplishment, one parent became famous among the elementary school teachers at my school. Over the teachers' expressed prohibition, the parent presented the trophies as a surprise on the last day of school. The children didn't seem to understand the gesture. At the end of the day, some of the children didn't even take the trophies home. I played football on a small college team that had the longest winning streak in the nation for a college its size back in the late '60s. When my daughter was in the fourth grade she played on a weekend soccer team, which did not have a winning season. I was surprised to learn that the league registration fee included the presentation of a trophy to every player in the soccer league at the end of the season. The trophy she brought home is twice the size of mine.

It is not only our young children who are getting confused messages. After a meeting of parents of seniors who were planning a post-graduation party for their sons and daughters, a mother came to me quite upset. She was appalled that such extravagant arrangements would be made to celebrate graduation from high school. She said, "Most people don't have a wedding day with such lavishness." The party was not an official school function, and she knew I had no control over it. She simply wanted to vent her frustration; she knew I would be sympathetic, because I had already publically expressed my concern about these events. She was a sensible woman who simply wanted to keep the events of her daughter's life in proportion. She was out-voted by a group of parents who wanted to append additional meaning to an event that needed no embellishment, and the party went on as planned. By all accounts, the party was spectacular. However, the graduates reportedly left the grand occasion after only one hour, and the parents who planned the expensive party were left wondering why their children didn't seem to appreciate their efforts.

By such misguided gestures, children in our society get very confusing messages. We honor children when we lovingly apply restraint, first by applying it to ourselves, and then by applying that same restraint to our children. It is like the advice we get on airplanes: "In case of an emergency, put on your own oxygen mask before you assist your child."

In the Scripture, law comes before love. St. John writes, "The law indeed was given through Moses; grace and truth came through Jesus Christ" (John 1:17). This means that before the love of God could be fully shown to the world in the gift of God's son Jesus, the law of God had to be given to us. The Old Testament embodies the law of God; the Gospel, God's gracious love. It is in the wisdom of that order of God's gifts that we parents ought to take special note.

If you asked most people, "Do you love your children?" they would say, "Yes!" But, if you asked them, "How do you love your children?" they may be a little confused by the question. How to love a child is one of the greatest challenges a parent faces. The greatest gift of love to a child might not be what we give them nor what we say to them, but simply what we show them.

A wise pastor and counselor once told me that when it comes to children, the best approach is one of maximum love and minimum control. He knew that neither love nor control alone was sufficient to rear a healthy child. He also knew that the techniques used to control the behavior of children were most often incidental compared with the principles upon which those techniques were based. He was a wise man. He knew that parents must struggle to keep a balance between these two important ingredients necessary for effective parenting. One without the other leads to disaster. The more difficult the child is, the more complex his or her needs are. The more complicated the family circumstances (divorce, separation, death of a parent), the more desperate parents may become. Even in the best situations, parents struggle to find ways of conveying love as well as values to their children. Most often the conflict over values between a parent and a child emerges not in abstract discussions, but in the child's behavior. Frequently, problems are exacerbated when parents cast about for ways to exercise more control over the child after love alone has not produced healthy behavior.

Loving Discipline

Scott Peck wisely observed in *The Road Less Traveled* that the problem with poor parenting "is undisciplined discipline."[6] Learning how to administer discipline lovingly and thoughtfully to children, discipline appropriate to each age and circumstance, is one of the great challenges of being a parent. Ultimately, we want our children to exercise principled self-control. Too often, the Bible's wisdom on the discipline of children is thought to be solely contained in the most quoted verse on the subject: "Those who spare the rod hate their children, but those who love them are diligent to discipline them" (Prov. 13:24). What parents often don't properly consider is that the self-control learned by a child is dependent on the parents' example rather than on any psychological manipulation of the child. "Do as I say, not as I do" has always been the quintessence of bad parenting, for children learn more from their parents' self-restraint than they do from the stringent imposition of rules.

Those standards of behavior which spring from the deeply held convictions of parents give children a sense of ownership of their own behavior. Often parents want behavior from children for which the children have not been prepared or which is beyond their ability to demonstrate. I once baptized a very active two-year-old (is there another kind?). There was no way the child was going to stand quietly while the pre-baptismal liturgy and prayers were read. I counseled the parents to allow the child freedom once they came up to the chancel area. The child's comfort level would increase with some familiarity, and because this age group is so self-absorbed, the child would be less self-conscious in front of the congregation if he was not restrained. Despite my admonitions, as soon as we assembled in the front of the church, the father began restraining the child. By the time I tried to hold the boy to baptize him, he was wild. Any two-year-old in a public ceremony is risky; however, suddenly demanding behavior and actions expected nowhere else in the child's life is stupid. In this case, the child's poor behavior in church was the parents' fault, not the child's. This loving father was guilty of undisciplined discipline.

Children should remain with parents during church services. Children should be removed if they become distracting but rewarded when they sit quietly. One week will build upon another until the entire service can be attended. Even though the words of the service may mean little, the sacred moment, the bowed head of his parents, and the idea that there is a time when parent and child stand equally before God, will leave a lasting impression. Being shipped off to Sunday school or choir rehearsal in the middle of the service does not build a tolerance to sacred space. Remember, worship is an acquired taste.

A first-grade teacher taught me about realistic expectations of children. At my school, we have a schoolwide lessons and carols service the day before we break for Christmas vacation. It is a glorious occasion where students from grades one through twelve gather with faculty and parents, sing beautiful Christmas carols, and listen to the account of the coming of the savior into the world. When we first planned the service, the elementary school faculty voiced concern that an hour's service might be too long for the younger children to sit quietly and listen to several passages from the Bible and to sing carols. However, I was adamant that students in all the grades attend. The first service began beautifully, but, as we moved through the series of nine Scripture passages, I became very much aware that the youngest students were making a good deal of noise. Faculty seemed to be doing their best to quiet them, but the squirming and shuffling continued. After the service, I spoke to one of the teachers from our elementary school division and said with all the self-righteousness headmasters are known for that I hoped next year we would better prepare the first graders by having them practice sitting still in a public assembly. She said, "If you hadn't instructed the ushers to give them programs as they entered the worship service, they'd have been quieter."

"I wanted even the youngest child to have a program and to feel a part of this special service," I retorted.

"But George, they can't read!" she said, and patted me on the shoulder.

She seemed certain that both the children and the headmaster would do better next year.

Parents and headmasters must learn to adjust to the changing needs of children. A parent's responsibility dwarfs that of any teacher because a parent's love is unlike any other kind of love. Most healthy relationships of love between adults are nurtured by the return of affection. However, all parents quickly learn that the love of a parent for a child is often unrequited. This one-way love is required of the parent for the tiny infant just as much as it is for the petulant adolescent. Our love for our children resembles God's love for us in that children can only see at any given moment a small fraction of the entirety of our love for them. To be a parent is to establish a relationship with the unborn which, at its root, is this commitment: "I will love you before I know you, and I will love you for always." As Jesus was sure God's love preexisted even the creation of the world,[7] our children must also be able to trust not only the preexistence of our love for them, but the sure promise of its uninterrupted continuation.

This commitment to love our children as God loves us, to love them no matter what becomes of them or whether they love us in return, should not be confused with what is popularly known as unconditional love. Conversely, the demands for obedience to God's law, which dominate the story line of the Old Testament, should also not be misunderstood as the biblical version of tough love. Tough love, which is designed to rein in a child's behavior once it is out of control, is often reserved for the recalcitrant adolescent, whereas unconditional love, we are told, is every child's right. God seems to disagree. A careful reading of the Bible suggests that popular culture might have this sequence backward, and that God gives us much better guidance on how to rear children.

The sequence of God's actions in Scripture tells us a great deal. There are two covenants between God and humankind in the Old Testament. The first is commonly referred to as the Mosaic Covenant, so named because it is captured in the spirit of the Ten Commandments, which Moses brought down from Sinai. God may have started with ten "words," but the priests and rabbis quickly elaborated upon God's work. When they were done, there were 613 laws in the Hebrew Bible: 365 "thou shalt nots" and 248 "thou shalts." As Professor Bernhard Anderson noted, all of these laws can be summarized: "Obey Yahweh and all will go well; disobey him and hardship will follow."[8]

The second covenant of the Old Testament, which is commonly known as the Davidic Covenant, is named to reflect the special relationship between King David and God. In this second covenant, Yahweh chose to limit divine power in a dramatic way. Instead of a covenant that required the recipient to keep the relationship going through obedience, in the Davidic Covenant, God promises to keep the covenant. That is, God promises to love Israel regardless of what happens.[9] Although David will be punished for his sins under the Mosaic Covenant, of the king's descendants, God promises, ". . . I will not take my steadfast love from [them]" (2 Sam. 7:15).

The Davidic Covenant changes the rules of the Mosaic Covenant. After David, obedience to the law would no longer be the condition for God's love and care; rather, God's love would be unconditional, and God would be the keeper of the covenant. This unfathomable gift of love promised to David for his heirs is manifested in the life and teachings of Jesus Christ and through him to all of us.

Why these two covenants appear in this order is profoundly important. God gives law first, and then unconditional love to God's children. God knew that Israel needed law first before it could comprehend the full nature of God's love. God knows that disciplining children is harder than loving them, because loving discipline requires more work on the part of the parent than does unconditional love. In fact, one might deduce from God's action that to truly love children first requires setting limits on one's self. Young children need the law consistently set before them through good examples, while it is the adolescent, over whose behavior we parents instinctively try to exert increased control, who really needs our unconditional love. This seems to run counter to modern conventional wisdom, but God's wisdom often does.

God's Confusing Question

One of the most powerful stories in the Bible is the murder of Abel by his jealous brother, Cain. Just before Cain kills his brother, God asks him a question that, at first, may sound rhetorical, but in reality may be one of the important factors responsible for this senseless tragedy. God asks Cain, "If you do well, will you not be accepted?" (Gen. 4:7). Two sentences later, Abel is dead.

What did God mean when God asked Cain this odd question? Could it have contributed to Cain's decision to kill Abel? In his brilliant commentary on Genesis, Walter Brueggemann offers a startling possibility:

> Life is not a garden party but a harsh fellowship among watchful siblings, made harsher by the heavy ways of God. The family would perhaps have gotten along better without this God.[10]

Brueggemann's reading of the story portrays God as capriciously creating a contest between two boys and implying dark consequences for one if the results aren't pleasing. When seen in this light, we might conclude that God contributes to the circumstances that lead to tragic results.

Cain kills Abel. The story is clear on that point, and we waste time try-ing to place the blame on God. Yet, we must consider the impact of this curious question. Is it possible that God has preserved this story for par-ents so that we might learn about the dangers of misinterpreted messages of love? To begin to explore this possibility, let us first review the facts of the story.

The story begins with Adam and Eve, fresh from the garden, with the curse of God for their disobedience still ringing in their ears. Two sons are born, Cain and Abel. We know nothing of the boys' childhood. All we learn is that, as they mature, they gravitate toward two different occupations. Cain takes up farming, and Abel herds sheep. Suddenly, the story shifts to a contest between the boys, which results in God receiving the sacrificial gift of one boy and rejecting the other's offering. Although why God chooses the sacrifice of one over the other is not made clear, the conse-quences are sudden and dramatic. Cain's jealousy over God's rejection of his sacrifice drives him to kill Abel.

The facts of this story are disturbing and contain an ancient harbinger of modern domestic tragedies made sensational in today's news stories. How-ever, like other stories preserved by the ancient writers of Genesis, it is the matter-of-fact way in which the story is told that makes it all the more chill-ing to the modern reader. Scholars tell us that all biblical stories can be read at three levels: the historical (How was this text first heard?), the traditional (What have the centuries made of it?), and the personal (How do you read the tale?).[11] The story of Cain and Abel is rich in each category. For exam-ple, at the personal level, this story has always resonated deeply and uncomfortably with every generation of readers, for who has not wished the death of his rival?

Traditionally, this text has been the focus of a complex theological debate about the origin of evil, or theodicy. Remember, Adam and Eve are punished for their disobedience in the garden, not for sin. Cain's act is the first real sin recorded in the Bible. In contrast to Adam's and Eve's simple disobedience, Cain's murderous act is motivated by evil. This story warns us that people set free by God will be capable of heinous crimes after the incidents in the garden.

The historical implications of this story, how the story may have been first intended to be read, may rest in traditional ethnic hatreds, which touch even our modern world. This story has been interpreted by some as an antecedent to the modern Arab/Israeli conflict. This link began when the ancient Israelite was a seminomadic herder and invaded the land of the ancient Canaanite farmers (today's Palestinians). Joshua and his Israelite forces, the Bible records, took the land from the Canaanites. To this day, land and power have remained at the heart of the conflict in the Middle East.

The biblical Israelite delighted in delivering the first blow of battle by renouncing his opponents and telling of their unworthiness. A good example of this strategy comes later in Genesis when the Israelites establish that their bitter Arab enemies of Transjordan, the Ammonites and Moabites, descended from the drunken and incestuous relationships between Lot and his daughters.[12] As the reasoning went, people with such unworthy heritage could hardly triumph over God's chosen people.

The difference between the farmer and the herder in biblical times is elemental. With the Iron Age (as early as 1350 B.C. in Egypt) came the plow and the ability to cultivate large tracts of land. The herder was an unpredictable intrusion into the orderly life of the farmer, for moving herds and families, often across cultivated land in search of water and grazing, destroyed much of the farmers' work. The conflict between the invading seminomadic Israelites into the farms of the Canaanites was as much of a cultural and economic clash as a military one. In the story, written about ancient times but codified after the conquest of Canaan, Cain represents his namesake, the Canaanite farmer, and Abel the invading Israelite herder. In the ongoing wars between ancient Canaanite and Israelite, the story of the treachery of the Canaanite farmer was fair warning to the Israelite to be wary of his Arab neighbor. Even after the Israelite became domesticated to the farm, the perfidy of the Canaanite was to be remembered by succeeding generations. In that sense, this story has never been forgotten.

I once visited Israel with an archeological group. One night, I was on my own in Jerusalem for dinner. I hailed a cab in front of the hotel, prepared with the names of restaurants recommended by the concierge. My driver was an Israeli. It was late when I started out, because I had been stood up. A friend had put me in touch with a fellow headmaster who was running a small school for displaced Palestinian children. I had spoken to the man by telephone and was supposed to meet him for dinner. I told him that I would wait for him in the lounge of the hotel, but he never arrived. I casually mentioned to the cab driver the reason for my late restaurant search, and he only laughed.

"You expected an Arab to get into *that* hotel?" he snorted incredulously.

I wasn't sure my fellow schoolmaster was an Arab. It had never come up in conversation. My driver snickered at my naivete. I said I would be upset with the hotel if my guest was not allowed to enter for a meeting with me. He pulled up to a traffic light and stopped the cab. He turned around in his seat and said gravely, "You Americans must understand, the only good Arab is a dead Arab." He turned around and drove on. We said nothing more. I learned later that the schoolmaster had, indeed, come to the hotel, but had been turned away at the door. Because he couldn't see me from the doorway, he wasn't permitted entry for "security reasons." The ancient controversies between Arabs and Jews are as old as the story of Cain and Abel. As one television correspondent said of the two sides, "They don't like each other; they don't believe each other; and they don't trust each other."[13]

In addition to the historical, traditional, and personal ways the story of Cain and Abel can be read, it contains a profound message for all parents. Look at the story from Cain's point of view. God may have said, "If you do well, will you not be accepted?" God may have meant, in effect, "Do your best." Tragically, however, without some greater clarification of what "do well" meant, Cain heard only, "Win!"

I remember vividly the exchange between a boy and his father in my office. The boy was in trouble for cheating on a test. The father was distraught at the dishonesty of his son. "I wanted to do well," was the boy's only defense. Unable to contain his anger, his father bellowed back at him, "All I have ever asked of you is that you do your best!" The boy meekly replied, "Do you know how hard it is to do your best all the time?"

Very often adults tell children what we think is a clear message: "Just do your best." In reality, what adult does his best *every* day? Adults have the option of saying, "I'm not good at math, so I'll have an accountant to do my taxes." Kids don't have that luxury. They must attend math class every day. I once heard an extraordinary coach at an awards assembly compliment her team for displaying a characteristic we sometimes underestimate in life. Her girls' tennis team had been successful, but she did not speak to the audience solely about its win/loss record. She told us of her high regard for the team because the girls were willing to try new things and to look silly doing them just because she, the coach, said that they would play better tennis if they trusted her guidance in practice drills. She said that, as an adult, she could often pick and choose what she would do and was often able to avoid difficult tasks that made her look less able. Her players' willingness to put aside their inhibitions and insecurities of adolescence was an admirable quality rarely found in adults. We parents often underestimate how difficult it is for youth to meet the vague "do well" standard or ambiguous "do your best" requirement in front of a world of peers ready to make fun of any mistakes.

God is not to blame for the contest between Cain and Abel. Cain's interpretation of God's message, however, is calamitous not only for Cain, but for us. I asked a boy one time why he had cheated on a test. I said, "You know the Honor Code, and you knew you would be thrown out of school for doing this." All the boy said was, "I was more afraid of what my parents would say if I didn't get a good grade than of what you would do if you caught me." Like Cain, that boy was willing to chance it all to win, for he had misunderstood his parents and believed that he had to win in order to be loved.

After showing us what a disastrous response we can get from children when they are uncertain how to attain parental affection, God shows us that there is a better way. In the very next book of the Bible following the story of Cain and Abel, God gives us the law, a very clear definition of what it means to "do well" in God's sight. Never again does a son or daughter of Adam and Eve have to be confused about God's expectations. God is never vague again. A wise parent should heed God's example, for it is one of the most important biblical principles of parenting. We must set clear expectations before our children and consistently demand their best effort to meet those expectations. When God gave the law, God gave more than clarity. God's great gift wasn't just a bunch of rules that God consistently applied to God's children. Extraordinarily, God too followed these same rules.

After Exodus, no longer would the deity's commands seem serendipitous to God's children, nor would they be subject to the *largess* of God. From the moment God gave us law, God gave us control over our lives. In the law, God directs us to the path to social tranquility, prosperity, social justice, and peace. No longer was the command a general "do well"; rather, it was a very specific "do this." God provides us parents with a good example in this action. Clear and consistent expectations, which are binding to both the child and the parent, give the child confidence. When law is built on love and applied mutually and consistently, the child knows she lives in an ordered, logical, and dependable universe, one in which she, too, can dare to love in return.

Let me be precise about the model that I think God is giving to us parents. When God is bound to people through the law, God is not subjected to indeterminate manipulation by people. God's ways remain higher than our ways. Just as certain prerogatives remain God's, so too should certain liberties remain for adults only. In other words, privileges such as driving a car, drinking alcohol, or having sex should remain adult prerogatives based on long-term commitments and emotional and physical maturity. Justice and love, on the other hand, should apply to all, regardless of age. Children should know that they have as much right to justice as do their parents. When "Thou shalt not bear false witness" is the standard upheld by parents in their dealings with children, the children come to value honesty and do not see personal integrity as a temporary burden of childhood. Children need to have set before them high expectations that are fairly and lovingly administered. Some parents hope that they can love a child so much that everything else will take care of itself. What these parents don't understand is that without well-defined expectations (the law), a parent's expressions of love may be delivering an unintended and very confusing message.

"I Just Want Them to Be Happy"

"Isn't there someone else you can recommend?" A very disappointed and frustrated father asked me this question one afternoon as we sat in my office. He was fresh from a family therapy session with his estranged wife and two young children. His frustration was palpable. Both of his children were students in my school, one in the middle school and the other in the elementary division. A contentious divorce had resulted in the children's teachers being drawn into the parents' disagreements. The court had imposed what it must have thought to be a solomonic living arrangement upon the family, an arrangement quite common in modern domestic judicial decisions. The judge had decided upon joint custody and that each parent would have the children for two weeks at a time.

Because the parents could not agree on a consistent approach to homework, the school had encouraged family counseling and recommended some therapists to help them resolve this division. The children's education was suffering, and a major philosophical disagreement between the parents needed to be resolved before progress could be made. The father was a self-made man, having achieved much by hard work. He credited his education with providing him with the skills and self-discipline that enabled him to take advantage of the business opportunities that had come his way. He wanted his children to study hard and not to rely on an inheritance, a gift that he felt only dulled one's competitive edge. He wanted his children to be able to do what he had done with his life. He wanted their inheritance to allow them to become philanthropists as he was now.

While at his home, the children went right to their homework after a snack. When they finished their homework, it was carefully checked by the father. Any errors required a repeat effort, and sloppiness was not tolerated. During his two weeks with the children, schoolwork became the priority. His children completed their homework assignments on time and studied for their tests. Even at the dinner table, the conversation centered around life at school.

Then came the two weeks with mom. She, by contrast to the father, felt that schoolwork was overemphasized. She thought children should enjoy life and explore their creative instincts. Her children would inherit plenty of money, so why ruin their childhood with a lot of unnecessary homework? They should concentrate on becoming interesting people, have fun, and enjoy the good fortune of being born healthy and wealthy.

The counseling was a trial for all. The day I met with the father followed a particularly traumatic session. The children had not gotten good report cards. With their ability, Cs were unacceptable to the father. The mother thought that their grades were fine and, besides, the school shouldn't grade young children so hard. In a moment of pique, the counselor had asked the father what he wanted for his children. The father told me that he responded, "I just want them to be happy." The counselor said, "Well, everyone but you is happy with Cs."

These children were being given very mixed messages, by the court and by their parents. The rules changed every two weeks; the definition of happiness changed; the definitions of success and acceptance changed.

Parents don't need to be divorced to give their children conflicting messages. Lack of structure and changing or inconsistently applied rules can result in a child feeling insecure even in a two-parent household. "Disney Dad" and "Monster Mom" create manipulative children who go to disparate extremes to win approval. We know in schools that the poorest teachers give confusing assignments. The poorest tests have confusing directions. By contrast, clarity and consistency are characteristics of good teaching and good parenting. God modeled these characteristics of good parenting and good teaching when God spoke from Mt. Sinai with simple directness on the subject of parent/child relationships.

Where Honor Begins

We teach our children how to honor us when we treat our parents, aged or demented as they may become, with respect. We encourage our children to respect us when we first respect them by giving them some power over their lives. Power is not license. Power over one's life comes to children when they know the rules that apply to them and when those rules are consistently applied. When parents keep the rules and the rules are based on a true sense of justice, not whimsy, children know they are respected, and they can grow self-confident. When we respect children, they feel confident enough to respect others. Most children who are bullies lack self-confidence first. They bully others because they need to constantly remind themselves that they have power.

This is how we love children. We first show our parents respect, and then we apply thoughtful rules to our children's daily lives that are based on a true sense of justice and love. Then the hard part begins: We model our rules. That is the formula of love God gave to us, and it is the same precious gift we can give to our children.

Ten Things Parents Can Do
to Teach Their Children the Concept of Honor

1. Don't punish children in anger.

2. Don't psychologize punishment. A simple correction can turn into something very hurtful when parents, out of their own frustration, say to a child, "What's wrong with you?"

3. Keep your rules for children clear and connected to civility (including manners), respect, and safety. Explain the rules carefully, and you won't have to explain the punishment at all.

4. The punishment of children should be consistently applied and of short duration. Inconvenience them, not yourself. Remember: "The problem with poor parenting is undisciplined discipline" (Scott Peck from *The Road Less Traveled*).

5. Encourage independence in your child. Offer them some distance before they ask. Tip: Those small hand-held walkie-talkies are a great invention. They can give a parent a little peace of mind everywhere from around the yard to around the mall.

6. The best way to show honor to your children is with your time. Quality time is all the time you are with your child.

7. When you speak to or interact with your parents in the presence of your children, remember, your children are watching and learning what you expect of them. As the prophet wrote: "Sow for yourselves righteousness; reap steadfast love" (Hos. 10:12).

8. Keep the rewards a child receives commensurate with the achievement.

9. Remember, God gave us Ten Commandments. We shouldn't need to give more.

10. Remember on your worst days that Jesus drove his parents crazy, too.

Chapter 7

The Triumph of *Timshel*

A young boy enters a public restroom. A drifter cuts his throat and then walks calmly out the door past the waiting grandmother, leaving the boy to die. We read these kinds of stories, hear them on the radio, and see them on television. They leave us numb. We promise ourselves to keep a closer eye on our children, reassure ourselves that this kind of thing probably won't happen in any of the places we go. Then we emotionally move on, knowing we will hear another story like this, waiting for the next horrific tale. What do our children think?

During the now infamous O. J. Simpson trial, when it seemed impossible to get away from the special reports on the courtroom antics, my daughter, then nine years old, informed me over dinner one evening, in a very worried tone, that O. J. Simpson lived in our town. I told her that Simpson lived in California, far away from Virginia, and she had nothing to fear from him. She insisted he lived near us. I could tell she was upset that I was amused and not taking her report seriously. As it turned out, a young friend of hers in school had recently moved from Los Angeles and had lived near where the murders had taken place. Frightened by what she had heard on the television and radio about O. J. Simpson and piecing those reports together with what her friend had said ("O. J. Simpson used to live near me") was enough for my daughter. It took some doing, but I finally established the location of Simpson's house. I wondered afterward how long she had been fretting about O. J. before she mentioned it to me. I must admit that, for a while, he seemed to live in all of our living rooms. The events we hear about through the news media are often brought home to us. Our children talk about these things at school and, frequently, they worry about them. However, they don't always talk about them to us.

The Gulf War was a good example. As a faculty, our youngest students surprised us by not wanting to talk about the impending attack on Saddam Hussein. We encouraged parents to discuss "Desert Storm" with their children and, in the upper grades, teachers regularly used the unfolding events to teach geography and political issues. We prayed for our troops in chapel. As a faculty, we were not sure what we should do to reassure and inform our students in the first through fourth grades, our five-to-nine-year-olds. Surely, they knew something about the events, but the lower-school teachers reported getting few questions from them in class. We faced that constant adult dilemma. Should we raise a matter to reassure our children or would raising it only plant fears in their minds?

On the day the U.S. invaded Iraq, we assembled the young children and explained that they were safe and shouldn't worry about what they might hear about the war. We told them if they had questions to feel free to ask their parents or teachers. However, throughout that crisis and the terrorist attacks on New York and Washington, our students asked remarkably few questions. We never figured out whether their reticence was because they really felt safe or because they, too, were so used to spectacular and horrific reports in the media every day that they just hardened to the news.

In light of increased terrorism, the frequency with which U.S. military power is used in the world, the media propensity to dramatize events, and the speed with which events happening around the world are beamed into our homes, we parents face an important question. In a world where events and people are often described as evil by politicians or the press, what do we tell children about evil, and how does evil fit into a world made by God?

In contemporary America, the finest articulation of the biblical view of evil came from a man who had seen a great deal of it. The Reverend Dr. Martin Luther King Jr. taught us that, although the human heart has the capacity for either good or evil, evil need not triumph. There remains in us the possibility of hope, for within each of us, despite the disobedience we inherited from Adam and Eve, lingers the image of the perfect God who is good and whose goodness can overcome any evil. He put it this way: "We must never forget that there is something within human nature that can respond to goodness, that man is not totally depraved: to put it in theological terms, the image of God is never totally gone."[1] This *imago Dei*, this persistent ability for the human spirit to respond with goodness to God's love, is the theological center of Christian hope. Dr. King believed that God's love was so powerful that when displayed by us, it could change the human heart. When the image of God is ignited within us and God's love is displayed through our actions, "even the worst segregationist can become an integrationist."[2] Paul put it this way: "Do not be overcome by evil, but overcome evil with good" (Rom. 12:21).

Within the teaching of Dr. King and Saint Paul is the assumption that no one is bound to evil, but through our choice and the power of God's love, good can triumph over evil. We need not feel helpless in the face of evil. Evil is not an irresistible force. Evil is not programmed into DNA, nor is it a psychological flaw.[3] The Bible teaches us that we can overcome our basic instincts and all the external forces of evil if only we believe in God and exercise the choice to act on that belief. The Prince of Darkness is powerless before God. Yet this is not what our children are being taught.

The study of human behavior is primarily in the hands of psychologists, sociologists, and political scientists, not theologians. Yet one aspect of human behavior remains a question for both the scientist and the theologian: Is human behavior most influenced by "nature or nurture" (our inner predisposition [DNA] or our environment)? Are we shaped primarily by the internal factors (our "nature") or by the external factors of our lives (what has "nurtured" us)? What role do factors like mental instability and poverty play in shaping a person's life? In short, do bad people really have choices? Should criminals be held accountable for what they do? These questions have dominated even public policy debates.

The criminal justice system, for example, reflects this paradox. On one hand, we believe that we can change the behavior of criminals. To that end, our prisons are often run by the Department of Corrections, which is charged with the rehabilitation of prisoners. We even call some prisons penitentiaries, as if they were filled with people truly sorry for what they have done and who are on the road to society's forgiveness. Yet, paradoxically, this same system administers the death penalty, the one punishment after which no earthly hope for redemption exists.

It seems the more we study the brain and learn about pathogenesis, the stronger the assumption becomes that our actions are controlled by our unique genetic make-up. It is possible, we are told, that genetics not only control hair color and susceptibility to certain illnesses, but possibly one's proclivity toward criminal behavior. Contemporary theologian Shirley C. Guthrie summarizes the theological implications of this question this way:

> The problem lies in two apparently contradictory truths: (1) Sin is universal and inevitable. There is no one who can *not* sin. (2) Nevertheless, every person is responsible for his or her sinfulness. All of us, in other words, are caught in the trap William Faulkner describes when he has a wise person in *Requiem for a Nun* say paradoxically about sin: "You ain't *got* to. You can't help it."[4]

Paul had the same feeling. He wrote:

I do not understand my own actions. For I do not do what I want, but I do the very thing I hate. (Rom. 7:15)

Who the Devil?

Whether the devil is portrayed as a little red guy with a pitchfork and tail or a Hollywood monster, our children should know that neither image is biblical. Elaine Pagels, professor of religion at Princeton University, tries to set the record straight in her book, *The Origin of Satan*. She writes:

> In the Hebrew Bible, as in mainstream Judaism to this day, Satan never appears as Western Christendom has come to know him, as the leader of an "evil empire," an army of hostile spirits who make war on God and humankind alike.[5]

Not specifically named in the Old Testament, other than as a member of the heavenly court, a very different kind of Satan existed in the ancient Jewish writings. Pagels writes, "The figure of Satan, as it emerged over the centuries in Jewish tradition, is not a hostile power assailing Israel from without, but the source and representation of conflict *within* the community."[6] She notes that the Greek term, *diabolos*, from which we get the word *devil* means "one who throws something across one's path."[7]

In the New Testament, Satan is the tempter who plagues Jesus in the desert, only to leave, biding his time for another opportunity. Even there, however, the devil or Satan is never shown to be more powerful than Jesus. "Christian tradition," Pagels writes, "derives much of its power from the conviction that although the believer may feel besieged by evil forces, Christ has already won the decisive victory."[8]

The Bible is clear: We bring evil into our world through the sin we choose. We create most of our own and the world's problems through our actions or inactions. Evil is not a deadly force of an alien empire battling for our souls, but, rather, a seductive slide, which if chosen by us, whisks us away from God. I suggest to my students that they think of the biblical idea of sin as a trajectory of ethical decision making. Because of greed, neglect, and self-pity, we humans often point ourselves in the wrong direction. If unchecked, we fire off in that wrong direction; we go on to make one mistake after another. Of course, it is possible for circumstances to occasionally conspire to aim us in the wrong direction. However, most of the time, we choose separation from God and consciously choose sinful behavior. We allow ourselves to be seduced. We are like the drunk who chooses to drive. What happens next can hardly be called an accident.

Our job as Christian parents is to call our children to higher ways, to a higher trajectory of decision making, so that they might be able, in time, to make good decisions on their own. We are asking our children to choose to rely on the victory of Jesus to give us power over the challenges in our life. As the prophet Micah wrote:

> He has told you, O mortal, what is good;
> and what does the LORD require of you
> but to do justice, and to love kindness,
> and to walk humbly with your God?
>
> (Mic. 6:8)

It is the adult modeling of justice, love, and humility before God that teaches the child the right way. Without God, we are aimed in the wrong direction.

Timshel

The idea that we are free to choose between good and evil is beautifully captured in the biblical story of Cain and Abel. Cain's choice was a major theme of John Steinbeck's book *East of Eden*. In one of the most powerful scenes in the book, an old Chinese wise man who has studied the story of Cain for the first time discovers how important the wording of Genesis 4:7 really is:

> The American Standard translation *orders* men to triumph over sin. . . . The King James translation make a promise in "Thou shalt," meaning that men will surely triumph over sin. But the Hebrew word, the word *timshel*—"Thou mayest"—that gives a choice. It might be the most important word in the world. That says the way is open. That throws it right back on a man. . . .
>
> "Thou mayest"! Why that makes a man great, that gives him stature . . . , for in his weakness and his filth and his murder of his brother he has still the great choice. He can choose his course and fight it through and win. . . .
>
> It is easy out of laziness, out of weakness, to throw oneself into the lap of the deity saying, "I couldn't help it; the way was set." But think of the glory of the choice! That makes a man a man. A cat has no choice, a bee must make honey. There's no godliness there. . . .
>
> This is not theology. I have no bent toward gods. But I have a new love for that glittering instrument, the human soul. It is a lovely and unique thing in the universe. It is always attacked and never destroyed—because "Thou mayest."[9]

The biblical message is that whether in Kosovo, Columbine, or Kabul, it is within our collective power to overcome evil in any form. Adult overreaction to these tragedies has begun a new kind of witch-hunt targeting youth who dress oddly or whose attention-getting behavior seems more sinister in light of Littleton. These desperate measures and hand-wringing will be unproductive. As I discussed in chapter 1, children without a spiritual grounding often find little reason to live. It should not be surprising then that those same children see little reason for others to live either. What should be most troubling to parents and those of us who work with young people is that the friends of these killers seemed so ill-equipped to intervene before the killing began. The death threats and the ominous Web site seemed to give no clue to the young people who knew the killers before they killed. They saw evil and didn't recognize it or felt powerless before it.

A discussion of the issue of evil may sound too vague and amorphous to be practical to parents. It is, however, a mistake for parents to underestimate how important this issue is to children.

One year, despite the fact that the school I head has a long tradition of daily life being shaped by an Honor Code, we experienced a rash of stealing in the Upper School. In some ways, our Honor Code encourages a naivete on the part of students. We choose not to have lockers, backpacks are scattered around the school, and lacrosse sticks and other sports equipment are stacked in bins at the entrance. Stealing is rare among the student body, but the temptation is ever present. That atmosphere of trust makes us vulnerable to a thief.

Suddenly, money started to disappear from backpacks and purses. Even teachers were not immune. Sometimes large amounts were missing. Daily announcement periods, where the entire high school division met to announce club meeting times, sport contests results, and birthdays, turned into a series of angry reports of more thefts. The entire division was in an uproar. I received requests for lockable lockers and surveillance cameras from people whose confidence in the Honor Code had been shattered. The Honor Code came under attack from many corners; some faculty felt a real Honor Code could not exist in today's world. My job was even threatened. At a board meeting, several angry board members whose children had repeatedly lost money and valuable possessions demanded I do something. One even wondered aloud if the thefts didn't reflect a problem with weak leadership of the school. I was told to do something about this problem.

After the board meeting, several board members met with me to try to help. One offered to pay for a undercover detective to pose as a janitor to keep an eye on things. I shocked them when I said I would not take any extraordinary measures.

The next day I went to the student assembly. I told all the students that I had been directed to do something about the four-month-long string of thefts. I also told them that I had done all I intended to do. I had made as certain as I could that the thief was not on the evening cleaning crew. Also, I was sure no mysterious strangers were coming on campus during the middle of the day. It was clear to me that the thief was in the room, sitting among us in the assembly. This thief was stealing more than our money. He was stealing the spirit of our school. I suspected that at least one person in our upper school knew what the thief was doing. That person, who sat idly by, was truly evil because he or she was allowing someone to ruin the positive school culture. To sit by and do nothing was to do equal harm. I closed my comments by saying that until we are all unwilling to sit by, until the evil around us is exposed, we will all be mastered by it.

You could hear a pin drop in the assembly. I said nothing more and retreated to my office to wait.

Several days went by. Then, the director of the upper school called me. Acting on a tip, the president of the student body had organized a surveillance team of students during free periods to watch a backpack that had money in it, bills whose serial numbers had been recorded. When the planted money was taken, one of the members of the team identified the last person he had seen near the backpack. On the strength of the story, we called the suspected student from class. The student willingly turned over his wallet to us, assuming we had no way of knowing about his latest caper. The marked bills were there, and the boy was immediately dismissed. The thefts ended that day. Evil had been thwarted.

This is a small victory, and it may sound silly to compare an energetic petty thief to systematic killers; but, especially with young people, it is in the small lessons that the seeds of great acts are sown. The human spirit can be drawn to good, but goodness requires an advocate. We have our advocate in Jesus Christ. His truth is more powerful than any evil the world can muster. We must first believe in his power and then empower our children to confront the evil in their world. If we have confidence in God and confidence in our children, we all shall overcome.

The power God gave to Cain must be given to our children. "Thou mayest!" deputizes and gives authority over evil. Our children know what other children are doing. Our children must not shrink from what they see around them but must use the power given to them to intervene. As Paul admonished the Romans, we must empower our children:

Do not be overcome by evil, but overcome evil with good. (Rom. 12:21)

Walter Brueggemann, the Old Testament scholar, is very helpful to us in understanding Cain's choice:

> The first alternative, "to do well,"is instructive. It suggests that a post-Genesis man can do well (cf. Amos 5:15). He is not "fallen.". . . He can choose and act for the good.. . . Cain in this story is free and capable of faithful living.[10]

That is the essence of *Timshel*. Once we believe that the power for good is within our grasp and we tell our children about it, our children have a real option over the crushing hopelessness of rejection and an alternative to senseless violence. *"Timshel."*

Enmity

The murder of children rivets a parent with fear and raises the great questions of evil, but the truth is that the overwhelming challenges of parenting are not embodied in the mysterious evil strangers from whom we must protect our children. The constant dangers our children face are in the subtle but equally pernicious elements that silently creep into our children's lives. These modern corruptors of our youth don't always jump out of the darkness and attack; rather, we often unwittingly invite them into our homes through such benign vehicles as the television and the Internet. Like Proteus, evil is a master of disguise. Evil can be present even in such traditionally safe places as church groups and the Boy Scouts. I learned this from a former student.

I once received a telephone call from a young man who left my school many years earlier under a cloud of suspicion about drug use. Nothing had been proven at the time about his involvement with drugs, but rumors abounded before he left.

Students who operate in the drug world generally don't enjoy a very good relationship with school authorities. The young man's relationship with me was no exception. He had been confronted about our suspicions but had left school before anything was proven. Long afterward, I heard horror stories about his increasing involvement with drugs. Then I lost track of him.

When he called that day, however, he sounded like an old friend. "The school was the first to confront me about my drug use," he told me. "It took years for me to hit the bottom with a lot of hurt and pain along the way, especially to my family. I've got my life together at last, and I am trying to make it up to those who tried to help me. I know you take a lot of heat when you confront kids about their drug and alcohol use. I'd like to tell my story to the students and publicly thank you and the teachers for what you tried to do."

This was a schoolmaster's dream! Vindication! Perhaps we could prevent another life from being lost to substance abuse by having him tell his story to our high school students. A little public expression of gratitude to his old headmaster and the faculty couldn't hurt either. I quickly accepted his invitation.

In front of the students, he told a horrific tale of drug addiction, memory loss, estrangement from his family, disease, and homelessness. Yet, now he was back in college, his health had blessedly returned, and he looked very much like the young man I had known before he got into drugs—a handsome boy with a an easy smile.

As he leaned against the stage in the auditorium with a self-confident air, I was proud of the small role the school had played in slowing the journey that would have certainly led to this young man's death. However, as he got into the story, I became uneasy. Although he delivered the admonition against drugs to the students as promised, he also made an observation that absolutely floored me. He said, "My parents suspected something was wrong long before my teachers started to see signs in my work, so my parents forbade me from seeing my friends. They thought my friends were a bad influence on me. My parents restricted my non-school activities to the church youth group, which was O.K. with me because that was where I was getting my drugs."

One of the first stories in the Bible portrays evil as stealthily slithering into the lives of God's children while they lived in a beautiful and well-protected environment. Genesis reminds us that we must be on guard against evil in all its forms, whether lurking in the dark, at a church youth group, or on the Internet. We will not always be there, and God knows that the really important battles will not be fought by the parent on behalf of the child, but by the child alone:

The LORD God said to the serpent,
"Because you have done this, cursed are you among all animals
and among all wild creatures;
upon your belly you shall go,
and dust you shall eat

all the days of your life. I will put enmity between you and the woman,
and between your offspring and hers;
he will strike your head,
and you will strike his heel."

(Gen. 3:14–15)

Often the cursing of the serpent in the Genesis account is dismissed or
glossed over as cultural mythology, explaining why most people don't like
snakes. The snake, by the way, later makes a comeback when Moses ele-
vates it in a bronze version wrapped around his staff as a symbol of healing,[11] an emblem still used today by the medical profession. However,
I think the curse God places on the snake deserves some deeper consideration by parents as we prepare our children to face the forces of evil in
their lives.

God's judgment on the snake is: "I will put enmity between you and the
woman, and between your offspring and hers." The word *enmity,* a word
not much used in modern English, has its root in enemy. God makes the
snake an enemy of God's children and their children. Notice that God does-
n't attack the snake and kill it. God doesn't make a law against snakes. God
doesn't even interrogate the snake to expose his involvement. Rather, God
draws God's children into the matter, arming them for their future battles
with evil.

One of our modern child-rearing problems is pornography on the Internet. During the 1996 presidential campaign, the candidates promised a
magic V-chip, which we could simply install in every computer to keep sexually explicit and predatory material out of the hands of our children. This
idea revealed how naive our politicians are about emerging technologies.
The V-chip promise also reveals how little we have learned from Genesis.
God could have blamed the snake, or put a V-chip in the serpent to prevent
it from interfering with God's plan for the future, but God knows the futility of killing the messenger, even if our politicians don't.

Don't Kill the Television

"We don't allow television in our home, but my seven-year-old daughter
watches it when she visits friends. How do I tell the parents of my daughter's friends that I would rather that they not allow my daughter to watch
television when she visits their homes?"

A caring parent asked this question following a presentation I made on
Christian parenting. During my talk, I had been critical of parents who use

the television as a babysitter. I told the audience that I find it irresponsible for adults to expose a child to the venality of this popular media without careful adult supervision, yet the vast majority of the time children watch television with no adult present.

Mistakenly, the person asking the question assumed I was against children watching any television. I surprised the parent when I queried, "Why don't you let your child watch television?" The parent defended her point by explaining how horrible the programming was and how deleterious the sex and gratuitous violence was that permeates many television shows. I understood why she didn't want her child exposed to such repulsive behavior.

I am not, however, against children watching television. I don't advocate that parents "kill the television," as the bumper sticker suggests. Rather, I think parents should watch television with their children. Television is too powerful a medium for parents not to take an active role in shaping and sharpening a child's television-watching skills. A colleague of mine maintains that because of the power and pervasiveness of television, teaching media criticism is a more important skill for young people to have than skill in literary criticism. By watching television with our children, no matter their age, we are giving them an important skill and good messages. First, we can teach them to be critical of what they watch. Second, we are acknowledging the positive potential of television. Like all good things in life, it takes time to develop a discriminating palate. Good programming is not easy to find, but it does exist. Parents must be willing to do the work of searching for good examples of positive programming. While creating enmity between our children and the trash on television, we must also help them create an affinity for the good options available.

How we spend our time teaches our children a great deal about what we believe. For this reason, I always compliment parents who attend Parents' Night at school. I say to them that they have sent their children a positive message by coming home from work, racing through dinner, and rushing out the door to spend an evening with their children's teachers. By making that effort, we are saying with our actions, "school is important."

We must apply that standard to what *we* watch on television. No matter how clandestine we are, our children see snippets of what we watch. Sometimes they hear only faint echoes of television dialogue or sound effects from their bedrooms. However, they do know more about our television habits than we think. They follow closely what we do because they are curious about us, want to be like us, and desire the power over their lives that we seem to have over ours.

I once talked with a father who was very concerned that his son didn't like to read. The boy had just entered the middle school and never read beyond homework assignments, which were completed only grudgingly. The father was concerned that, by not liking to read, the boy would lack the proper academic skills to succeed in school. The father had bought the boy *Sports Illustrated* subscriptions, even comic books, to encourage his reading—all to no avail. I asked the father, "Do you like to read?" "Yes," was his immediate reply. "Does your son see you read?" This time the answer didn't come as fast. The father confessed that, during the time his son did his homework at night, he usually watched television. The father also noted something unusual. He said that he rarely finished a book. He said that he often grew impatient with the pace of books and, for that reason, could rarely stick with them to the end.

His son watched him, and he watched television. How could the boy hope to develop the challenging skill of reading well when it looked like becoming an adult meant you didn't have to finish a book? Parents do not always calculate the impact of their example on their children. Remember, Jacob referred to the "God of my father." Jacob received not only his faith from his father, but the message that God was an important part of life. If you want your child to be a reader, make sure that he sees you reading. If you want your child to believe in God, take him to church and let him watch you worship God. This is why I prefer children (if their behavior permits) to remain in the sanctuary during worship services. They may not understand the words being said, but they are listening carefully to the silent examples of adult behavior.

If you want your children to learn what is good on television, sit with them and look together for a program. Use the mute, not only the on/off button. Stop the sound to discuss with your child what you are watching. Often, the television can serve as a good tool for thoughtful dialogue about values as well as aesthetics with children, but television and the Internet require vigilance. No good school allows unsupervised access to the Internet. Why should we permit it at home? What confounds me are the parents who allow their children to have unsupervised time on the Internet as a reward for good behavior. What the kids might be doing, even unwittingly, on the Internet may be undoing all the good lessons a parent has taught.

Another message you are giving your child when you watch television together is that you are not afraid of the bad messages that are on television. If a violent scene comes on, mute the sound and talk about what you've just seen. Explain why you object, why that dramatic action is not part of your family's values. Don't be intimidated by television sex, violence, and language. Of course, try to avoid programs that wallow in the sensational, but when objectionable material comes on—and it comes on even during otherwise acceptable shows—mute the sound and talk about it. If you decide that you must ban a television show, tell your children what your reasons are and ask for their agreement and compliance. To be armed with understanding and to have been shown that their parents are not afraid of the messages that television offers shows children that you believe in God's power. Such an approach can eventually create enmity between your child and the forces of evil in modern media and technology. When you give your children the judgment skills they can use when you are not sitting next to them, you have given them a gift they can use all their lives. Some children will reject this approach; others will defy you. Remember, young people continue to report that their parents are the most important influences in their lives. We can influence them and create an enmity between them and the snakes of the world.

The Good Book

Martin Luther wrote, "a child of nine if it has faith" can understand the Bible.[12] Luther raises an important point for parents to think about. When should our children read the Bible on their own? It may seem odd that in a chapter about evil, I would discuss children's literature or that, after pages of encouragement for parents to teach children the truths of Scripture, I would I raise this question. It may surprise you all the more then that I believe the Bible isn't for young children!

The Bible is a graphic, earthy book. In the Hebrew Bible, women deceive their fathers by faking their periods, daughters have sex with drunken fathers, men seduce other men's wives, and the murder of a husband is arranged as a cover-up. The Gospels aren't much better. Followers of Jesus are stoned, and the innocent Son of God is nailed to a cross, desperately pushing himself up by his nailed feet to gasp air before he dies. My students are always horrified at the description of Jesus' death, for often the event has been sanitized for them, especially in the liberal Protestant churches. At least in the older Catholic churches, graphic crucifixes often are prominently displayed as a reminder of the pain our Lord endured.

When do we tell our young children that Jesus probably died from a combination of suffocation and shock? When do we read the story of Jonah being swallowed by an enormous fish or Saul committing suicide? A young mother told me of the disconcerting experience of reading a beautifully illustrated book of Bible stories to her two-and-a-half-year-old before bed. The story was of Noah, and the brightly illustrated pages depicted in great detail the famous flood. The mother said her child cried inconsolably for hours after the session. The pictures of the sad animals, with only their noses and trunks above the water and with tiny birds perched on the ends of each, watching Noah and his selected few sail away, was just too much for the sensitive child. The mother told me, "No more Bible stories at bedtime in my house!" When and how do we tell our youngest children Bible stories?

The vast majority of the stories of the Bible started as oral tradition. No part of Scripture had illustrations in its original form. For young children, the simplest stories should be told to them without confusing or figurative drawings. The stories alone are powerful; they don't need an artist's help. Besides, the graphic details can unnecessarily scare young children. Even worse are the sanitized cartoon renderings, which only drain the profundity from the stories. My advice to parents is to just read the Bible yourself and tell the stories, in your own words, to young children. Ask them afterward if they have any questions and answer their questions the best you can. You serve the Lord well by inviting the young to think about matters of faith free from disconcerting details or pictures, which only block the fluid musings of the young.

About age nine, but certainly during the middle school years between the ages of ten and thirteen, children ought to be systematically introduced to the text of Scripture itself. In the middle school years, the biographies of the main characters in Scripture should be read and discussed. By that age they are ready for the details and, in fact, are usually impressed with them. The graphic scenes of the Old Testament often thrill this age. When the tent peg sinks into Sisera's temple,[13] Scripture is elevated in the mind of the middle-schooler to the ranks of Stephen King's best.

When full abstract thinking occurs, which often is not until the latter years of high school, the subtle metaphors of the Bible can engage the adolescent's new reasoning powers. Poorly prepared Sunday school teachers often miss opportunities to open the beauty and wisdom of scripture to this age group because they don't know the material well enough themselves. For all children, there is no substitute for a well-prepared and enthusiastic teacher. This is especially true for the teachers of adolescents. The church must do a better job of properly training those who teach our children. Good teaching gives children wings that can carry them on their own intellectual and spiritual journey. Unfortunately, our children are not usually taught well or inspired in church school. In public school, they are robbed completely of the opportunity to study Scripture as a faith document. We are rearing another generation of biblically illiterate young people, all of whom have been saved from the brainwashing that public officials fear they would undergo if they studied the Bible. Yet, one generation after another emerges from the classrooms of this country hungry for something more meaningful in their lives.

Ten Things Parents Can Do
to Give a Child the Power of *Timshel*

1.   The greatest power evil has is the power to make us think it doesn't exist.

2.   Don't psychoanalyze evil. Yes, some bad things are done by people who are sick or deranged. However, not all bad things have a psychological or genetic origin. Whatever the cause, there is real evil in our world. However, we can reassure our children that God has given us power over it, no matter its origin. Teach children that it is not in the falling down that life is lived, but in the getting up.

3.   Tell children that evil comes into our world most often as a trip-wire or what the Bible calls a "stumbling block." Evil is not usually a dark force that unexpectedly attacks us; rather, it is something placed in our path that brings us down because we haven't been watchful.

4.   The devil doesn't wear a red suit or carry a pitchfork. Rather, when the devil is at work, it looks a lot like you and me.

5.   Tell children that without God, our lives can get aimed in the wrong direction. With God in our lives, we are always on the right road.

6.   Tell young children Bible stories in your own words. Start formal Bible study after age nine.

7.   When our children encounter setbacks in their lives, reassure them with Paul's words: "Do not be overcome by evil, but overcome evil with good" (Rom. 12:21). We have the power!

8.   Watch TV with your children, talk to your children about it, and tell them what is often depicted as glamorous is really just the clever disguise of evil.

9.   Reading is always better than television.

10.   When your children disappoint you, remember that despite all that had been given to them God's first children chose the forbidden fruit. God loved them anyway, and that love led them back to God's ways in the end.

Chapter 8

The Spiritual Journey of Parenthood

Children challenge us. The defiant demands of the two-year-old, the relentless quest for independence of the young child, the powerful hormonal storms of the adolescent, and even the confused "twenty-something," all place different demands on us.

Children change us. They stir our deepest emotions, introduce us to fears we have never known, and test our resolve on almost everything that is important to us. They become our greatest joy, and they give us our worst nightmares. We live for them, and sometimes, we must learn to live on very little response from them. I tell couples whom I counsel before marriage that, as important as it is, the commitment they will make as a spouse on their wedding day pales in comparison to the commitment they will make if they become parents.

Children can overwhelm us. If there is a hurried child[1] in our culture, there are also many hurried parents. Many seem to rush along with their children from activity to activity, lesson to lesson, with very little time to reflect, enjoy, and grow. This approach to parenting is like the old television show where contestants were able to win minutes of free shopping time in a supermarket. Viewers were shown lucky players as they dashed madly around the market. Often the grocery basket tipped on two wheels as it and the contestants careened around the corners of the aisles, trying frantically to get as much as possible in the basket during the time allowed. As with parents of newborns, the optimism and anticipation of the contestants were palpable as they lined up for the race around the store. As time ran out, they became frantic and mere motion substituted for goal. On occasion, a great sigh of disappointment arose from the audience when the cargo spilled out of the lurching basket. Sometimes the whole cart turned over. The worst part was watching the contestant scrambling on hands and knees to salvage a few items before his time was up. That same frantic race seems characteristic of "grocery basket parents" who want to fill their child with good things before the basket tips over or time runs out.

The parents whose busy lives require scheduling every moment act like overworked executives. From these parents we now have the phrase "quality time" added to the parenting lexicon. These parents often must delegate parenting to others, and they are sorely disappointed when those who have been employed to rear their children let them down. I was once told by an angry executive parent that "if my child fails at your school, you have failed." Yes, when a child fails in school, the school shares the responsibility. However, the gentleman thought that purchasing a private school education ensured the child's success and relieved him of any responsibility. Failure would not be his fault. He had delegated the responsibility to me. If things didn't work out, subordinates were to blame.

Parents at war with their children fight a rear-action battle as they retreat from the romantic vision of parenthood. Usually these are good people who just happened to get a child who doesn't fit their preconceived notion of parenting. No matter the child's unique needs or accidents of birth, these parents cling to their approaches, trying them over and over again, like a soldier outnumbered and outmaneuvered. Life with children is a struggle for the soldier parent whose battle plan is in shambles but who seems committed to a single approach to parenting. One soldier parent looked me in the eye and said stoically, "She'll have to change; I won't." This was his response to my counsel that his bulemic daughter required a different kind of parenting as she struggled with her life-threatening eating disorder. Although this father loved his daughter, he was going to continue to fight using his failed strategy, even if his daughter was a casualty.

Tragically, the grocery basket parent, the executive parent, and the soldier parent all start with the same enthusiasm, but things just don't turn out the way they planned. What causes parents to get caught in these unsuccessful child-rearing practices is not lack of effort or love of their children, but a lack of spiritual depth. There are many different kinds of effective parenting and many different kinds of successful family structures, but there is one indisputable truth about being a parent. The Nobel Prize winning author Luigi Pirandello put it this way:

> Our children are born because. . . well, because they must be born, and when they come to life they take our own life with them. This is the truth. We belong to them but they never belong to us.[2]

God, above all, knows this truth. So, God captured an important lesson for us in Scripture. As Jack Miles observed in *God: A Biography*: "At the beginning of Abraham's story . . . , Abraham belongs to the Lord; at its end, the Lord belongs to Abraham."[3] That is the essence of a parent's love. As in no other kind of loving relationship, to love a child is to give oneself away. But, how can being a parent contribute to our spiritual growth?

We have discussed the spiritual inheritance we must give to our children in order for them to become spiritually healthy and emotionally resilient adults. The challenges of being a parent in the twenty-first century promise to be great. No matter what lies ahead, our children will still be our greatest joy and sometimes our greatest heartache. Parenting will remain a juggling act, full of managerial mountains to climb. We will have to be flexible and adapt our techniques to the child's needs and society's pressures. Like all good parents before us, we will have to stand firm on the principles we hold dear when we are responding to the needs of our children and the seductive coercions of our culture and the dangers of the world.

Being a parent should be more than a simple journey with our children toward their maturity. To give birth, to bring forth life, is to stand in the footsteps of God. Just as the creation of life began a spiritual relationship between God and God's children, so too does the relationship with our children begin a new spiritual phase of our life. Children come in all emotional shapes and sizes. Their needs vary enormously, but each brings a spiritual quality. All children, at every age, can be catalysts for their parents' spiritual growth.

The personal spiritual growth of a parent requires the use of some muscles we might not have exercised much in our life. The most effective spiritual exercise program is an old one called *Lectio Divina* or "reading divine things." It is a technique of spiritual exercise that can be easily adopted to the unique needs of parents. Professor Diogenes Allen of Princeton Theological Seminary is one of the most helpful of contemporary writers on this subject. Professor Allen shows how a nearly sixteen-hundred-year-old spiritual discipline, sometimes referred to in its modern manifestation as spiritual centering, can speak to us today. He writes:

> *Lectio Divina* consists of four interlocking parts: reading a passage of scripture to yourself aloud; meditating or thinking about what you have read; praying about what has risen up in your mind and heart in meditation; and then contemplation—simply resting silently in God for a time after you have prayed.[4]

Reading Scripture and thinking about it from the perspective of a parent has been the subject of previous chapters. The Bible contains a great deal of insight that parents can draw on once given the tools to mine its wisdom.

However, praying as a parent requires us to open ourselves up to God and the possibilities of change.

The purpose of prayer is communication with God. It is vitally important that we understand how prayer works. Prayer is not calling God with our problems. It is not that kind of communication because God already knows our needs: "Your Father knows what you need before you ask" (Matt. 6:8). Prayer helps us listen to God. In an age of instantaneous communication, patiently waiting for our prayers to be responded to in a way we recognize can make God seem very far away.

A Parent's Prayer

Prayer can buoy the human spirit, lifting it up to God's ear. As one child responded after his mother assured him that God hears everyone's prayer: "God must have big ears!" God does.

Jesus taught his disciples how to pray. Jesus' words structure Christian reflection on life. However, the Lord's Prayer is particularly powerful as a way for parents to reflect on the challenges and the changes children bring into our lives. In fact, the Lord's Prayer might very well be called the parent's prayer, because it so beautifully captures what is most important for parents to think about. Let us look at Jesus' prayer with new eyes, the eyes of a parent, and see how this familiar prayer can contribute to our spiritual journey.

First, Jesus is very directive when he teaches his disciples this prayer: "Pray then in this way: Our Father in heaven . . ." (Matt. 6:9).

Second, by stating emphatically how we are to pray, Jesus is allowing us to not only use the words of the prayer but also its structure for other prayers. The traditional form of the Lord's Prayer follows the typical synagogue prayer of Jesus' day: adoration bracketing petitions. "Hallowed be thy name" and "for thine is the kingdom and power and glory" are praises with which a Jew glorified the almighty Deity. Between praising God are four petitions in Jesus' prayer.

"Give Us This Day Our Daily Bread"

Why bread? Why not water? Water is more important than bread for sustaining life. Why, conversely, is Jesus so narrow in this petition? Why not use a broader category like sustenance? With sustenance, he would have been linking God to our every need.

The answer to these questions lies in the use of bread as a metaphor.

Jesus illumines a critical part of this metaphor when he describes the kingdom of heaven:

> He also said, "The kingdom of God is as if someone would scatter seed on the ground, and would sleep and rise night and day, and the seed would sprout and grow, he does not know how. The earth produces of itself, first the stalk, then the head, then the full grain in the head. But when the grain is ripe, at once he goes in with his sickle, because the harvest has come. (Mark 4:26–29)

Science knows a great deal about how things grow. We can alter how plants, animals, and even humans grow, but we cannot create life from scratch in any form. With all our knowledge, even the simplest DNA building block of life cannot be created. Like the biblical farmer, "the seed would sprout and grow, he does not know how." In a way, scientific manipulation of life is like the baking of bread. We can combine and recombine the ingredients, but we cannot make even one sprout of wheat.

This first petition of the Lord's Prayer is most important for parents to pray about. A pivotal precept of parental spiritual growth is that we are to accept our children as a gift from God. With that acceptance, and the reminder of this simple truth each time we pray, we come to understand that God has already created and given to us in our child the essential ingredients of who that child will become. We can't change the ingredients; we must accept God's gift as it is given. However, we are not passive players in this drama, we have an important role. We bake the bread from the ingredients God has given us. Thus, the bread metaphor becomes especially important for parents to consider. Remember, Jesus' phrase is "daily bread." We must pray daily for God's guidance in rearing our children. Each day is important. Each day we contribute to the formation of our child. Parenting cannot be confined to weekends or holidays.

We make a mistake when we confuse God's work with our own. It is futile to try to bake the loaf in our image. I remember a very intelligent and loving father of a fifth-grade boy who came to my office to discuss his son's performance in school. The father was very upset about his son's poor grades. The boy's lackadaisical attitude toward school deeply troubled him, for the father was a hard-working, accomplished architect. Why hadn't the virtue of hard work become a part of his son's life?

I told the father that his son was not doing well in school because he and his wife were doing the boy's homework. The evidence the teachers had given me was convincing. The homework assignments were done with draftsman-like precision. However, daily in-class work was haphazard and showed no signs of any of the knowledge or care displayed in the homework. It was clear that the parents would not let the boy fail. I told the father that the boy must do his own homework and get help only when he really needed it.

The father's emotions transformed from embarrassment to anger. He would not let his son fail. The father looked at his hands folded on the table in front of him and said, "I don't think we are going to get through the fifth grade." I said, "You already have, now let your son." This father's love didn't allow room for failure or social setback. This father was trying to make his son into one of the jewels in his crown of successes. What the boy really needed was a father, not a ghost writer.

We play an important role as a baker in the child's life. Our Maker has a plan for each of us, including our children. Our children are not monuments to us. When they fail, it doesn't mean we have failed. This is not to say that we should not cajole, assist, and encourage them at each step of life. We must accept the gift God gave to us and grow from it. One very accomplished woman once said to me of her very intellectually limited son, "God gave him to me so I could learn a deeper love than my other children have required of me." It is better to accept children for who they are and what they are: a gift from God for our spiritual growth.

"Forgive Us Our Debts as We Forgive Our Debtors"

Jesus tells us that we will be forgiven in the exact same proportion that we forgive. There aren't many other equations like that in Scripture. For parents, this is a particularly important petition to ponder. I often wonder why children, particularly during the middle school years, seem so reluctant to forgive or ask for forgiveness. Yes, all this might be a result of their growing self-consciousness, but I think there is more. Is it possible that our reluctance to ask for forgiveness of children sends a message that to forgive is to be weak? When we hear public officials acknowledge that "mistakes were made" or that their behavior was "wrong," yet they ask for no forgiveness and offer no apology for their offences, we must remember that our children are listening carefully. Perhaps it seems to them that in adulthood you have a greater selection of excuses to choose from.

Have you ever asked a young child to forgive you? Young children almost never say "no" to such a request. Oddly enough, parents are often reluctant to ask children for forgiveness. Perhaps we think that somehow we will be diminished in our child's eyes if we admit our mistakes. Our children learn how to receive forgiveness from us, but often do not learn how to give it. To be unable to forgive is an emotional handicap. Jesus reminds us in the Lord's Prayer that in order to receive forgiveness for our sins, we must forgive others. When children are put in the position of granting forgiveness to adults, they learn the great personal blessings that come to one who forgives another. We must remember that it is through granting forgiveness that children learn to forgive.

"Lead Us Not into Temptation"

Through prayer, we parents can learn how to avoid the peculiar temptations of parenting. Most of the problems that have visited my life I have brought on myself by actively "looking for trouble," as my mother used to say, or by not calling a halt to a series of events that I knew to be leading me in the wrong direction. The third petition of the Lord's Prayer, "Lead us not," reveals one of the most fundamental insights that Scripture gives. Resisting temptation begins with resisting visiting temptation.

I once heard a sermon illustration about a valuable coin that a father had given his son before the young man went off to college. The father said, "Take this, it's for an emergency. Use it if you ever get in trouble and need money to keep you safe. Don't spend it unless you really need it, and don't take it any place you wouldn't take your mother and me." The speaker said that he carried that gold coin with him throughout college like a cross! Each time he felt it in his pocket, he remembered what his father had told him, and he credited the admonition that the coin represented with helping him stay out of trouble throughout his college years.

There are tremendous temptations in parenting. We are granted control over a young life. Upon the child's birth, we become an intimate, daily teacher and role model. Over the years, I have hired many teachers. Even the very best usually weren't stars the first year. Perhaps this is what a very good mother meant when she told me that children are like pancakes: You ought to be able to throw the first couple away! It's not the pancake's fault; the cook gets better with experience. Regardless of whether or not the parents are teaching good lessons, what most young people take with them into future relationships they learn from their parents. Controlled and manipulated children learn to control and manipulate others. When parents pray this third petition, we are acknowledging that the path to the temptation of being a poor role model for our children is ours to take or reject.

"Deliver Us from Evil"

Finally, we return to the issue of evil. The word *deliver* has evolved in English to have a variety of meanings. Here *deliver* is used as an intransitive verb; as in, "the child was delivered." The *liver* part of the word comes from the Latin *liber,* "to free."[5]

If we understand evil[6] not as a camouflaged malevolent force that stalks us, but rather as the Bible portrays it, as something thrown across our path by the Tempter, then our petition to be freed from evil is a prayer to be protected from foolishly and clumsily stumbling. In other words, Jesus is drawing a distinction in separating the third and fourth petitions in the Lord's Prayer, between the trouble we get ourselves into (temptation) and the trouble not of our doing that trips us up (evil). When parents pray for God to "deliver us from evil," we are asking for the sight to see the bad things in life before we stumble over them. Here again, we are acknowledging our dependence on the power of God to protect us and our children, and recognizing our inability to create a trouble-free path through life for our children.

The Lord's Prayer provides a reliable vehicle for us to use as we reflect upon what we read in the Bible and upon the challenges of being a parent. As I told the young middle school students I mentioned in this book's introduction, the most effective way to feel close to God is through reflective prayer. Prayer is more than meditation. Reflective prayer is when one takes a moment to look back upon the day and think about the events that took place. When did we feel closest to God, and when did we feel farthest away? The Lord's Prayer gives us the structure within which we can gain the most from this daily reflection. In this exercise, we gain some notion of God's presence in our lives. As day builds upon day, a pattern of God's presence in the events of our lives emerges. Sensing God's presence brings peace and confidence to our parenting.

Anger

There is, however, a dark side to parenting. Sometimes the demands of being a parent wear people out. Stalled careers, enormous financial responsibilities, and strained marital relationships can visit parents even under the happiest circumstances. The divorce rate among parents of children with handicaps is staggeringly high. The strain of parenting a healthy child can be substantial, but the challenge of parenting a child with special needs is overwhelming for many. God knows these feelings and has given us some help in handling them.

"I am sorry that I have made them" (Gen. 6:7)

God decided in Genesis to destroy every ungrateful living thing. The story of Noah, the great flood, and the saving ark memorialize what happened when God's anger burst forth. The Genesis account tells us that the behavior of God's children was appalling; their ingratitude made God furious. After describing God that way during presentations, I simply ask my audience, "Ever feel that way about your kids?" Invariably, heads nod quietly at first, and then a little nervous laughter follows. To admit these feelings is not easy for most parents. We are not strangers to such feelings, but to admit to them somehow puts us in a league with the kind of people who hurt children. To admit to our anger toward our children exposes our most secret and taboo feelings. After my talks, I have had several parents tell me they were surprised so many people admitted feeling anger toward their children; they thought they were alone.

We must find productive ways of dealing with our anger toward our children, whether that anger manifests itself in the occasional aggravation any child evokes from a parent or whether it is the powerful exasperation some parents feel when they are completely at odds with their children. Adult anger released upon a child can be devastating for both. Pent-up anger that is unaddressed can eat at a person, corroding the positive aspects of his or her relations with others. The wise fourth-century monk, Evagrius, whom I introduced earlier, would counsel us to openly confront our anger, no matter how frightening it may be or how unnerving it may be for others to hear.

I wonder if that is what a friend of mine was doing one evening when he shocked an entire dinner table of friends. The night had been full of laughter, good food, and wine. We had told our old stories, embroidering new details on familiar tales for the entertainment of all. Each of us at the table had taught in a boarding school. A peculiar link binds boarding school teachers together, as does any intense and demanding experience. That evening we recounted tales of our first years as teachers, and the stories were hilarious.

We were conscious, however, that life had changed for all of us. We were older; children had been born, and a new school now employed us. Our conversation ranged from old friends and common experiences to family tales. At one point, our host momentarily stunned the table with an observation about his children. A good Christian man, a scholar, and a brilliant teacher of many years, the kind of teacher to whom yearbooks are dedicated, said of his three strong-willed young children, "I know how people feel who abuse their children; I have had all the same feelings. Sometimes I'd like to kill them. The only difference is, I don't do it! That's all. I have all the same thoughts!"

Exposing our deadly thoughts, naming them, is a powerful first step toward stopping them from moving from thoughts to actions. Evagrius taught that between the thought of a sin and the commission of a sin is a precious moment in which we have a choice. We have Cain's choice. We can act on our deadly thought or we can offer it up to God. In that moment, we have a choice.

Parenting is fundamentally a lonely task. Most of the challenges parents face are often faced alone. Those situations don't give us time to talk with friends or to discuss our feelings with a support group at church. Parenting can be an emotional roller-coaster. God knows this, so God gave us rainbows.

Rainbows

To understand the importance of rainbows in a parent's life, we must return to one of the oldest stories of the human race. The story of a great flood of the Bible has been preserved in different forms in many cultures. It is not the devastation of the flood, but God's decision to save Noah, that makes the biblical version of this story so important for parents to reflect upon. After the flood, the angry God who initiated this catastrophe imposed a restraint on this power in the future. God established a covenant with Noah and all humankind in God's promise to never again destroy the earth.

> I have set my bow in the clouds, and it shall be a sign of the covenant between me and the earth. When I bring clouds over the earth and the bow is seen in the clouds, I will remember my covenant that is between me and you and every living creature of all flesh; and the waters shall never again become a flood to destroy all flesh. When the bow is in the clouds, I will see it and remember the everlasting covenant between God and every living creature of all flesh that is on the earth. (Gen. 9:13–16)

God shared the emotions parents can experience when rearing children. Their behavior can disappoint us and make us angry. I was reminded of that when a parent of one of my daughter's friends called to make arrangements to pick up her daughter after a weekend overnight visit. In our conversation, I mentioned that her daughter had been a very polite visitor and she should be proud of the nice girl she had. The mother's reply was: "Tell me the truth, did she hang over her plate when she ate so that her hair dangled in her food like she does at home? She promises me she doesn't do that when she is out, but I don't believe her!" I assured her that her daughter kept her word. I could tell the child's rudeness at home made the mother angry, and I sensed she wished to see the "guest behavior" at home someday.

If there weren't more to it, God's full range of emotions from disgust to regret recorded in the flood story would be only cathartic. However, God gives us, through this story, a clue to triumphing over our anger toward our children. The rainbow is often thought of as a reminder to us of God's promise never to destroy the earth with another devastating flood. A closer reading of the text shows that the arch in the sky is not a reminder to us, but rather a reminder to God of God's promise. Notice the sixteenth verse from the passage just quoted: "When the bow is in the clouds, *I will see it and remember . . .*" (my emphasis). One of the most curious things about this passage is its lack of economy. There are several references to this new covenant with God's people. One wonders if the repetition, unusual in its number for the Hebrew Bible, actually could be God repeating these words, as a way of memorizing them.

The rainbow is God's example to us. God is teaching us to keep rainbows in our lives, reminders we can turn to, mementos that can help keep us from parenting's "deadly thoughts." "Rainbows" can be pictures of ourselves with our child at a special moment or a picture of our own parents with us. They should be reminders of the feelings that started our journey into parenthood. Special passages, poems, and letters can all serve as the rainbow we need to get us through the terrible twos, the impudence of adolescence, and the terrors of those midnight telephone calls when our teenager is not yet home.

Rainbows can help us choose another path during those moments between our deadly thought and a sinful act. I know a man who keeps his private office bathroom walls papered with notes, cards, and poems from his child. These rainbows cover the walls and reflect the child's work over many years. Each time he enters the room, he sees them and remembers. He thinks these daily reminders make him a better father. If God needs rainbows, don't we?

Rainbows can also make it easier when it is time to let go of our children. They can give us a history from which we can continue to draw both inspiration and solace. Without rainbow reminders, our children's growth can be very painful. One May, I came upon a mother of one of the seniors on a girls' lacrosse team after a championship game. We had won. We were the champions, but she was crying, and her tears were not tears of joy. I took her aside and inquired if I could assist her, but she could not be consoled. The game marked an end of a chapter in her life, and she couldn't see her life beyond her daughter's departure for college. She had doted on her daughter for years and had lived vicariously through every moment of the girl's life. The end of the big game had signaled the end of all that. She felt lost. She knew her child's senior year was coming to a close and the girl would soon be leaving the mother's nest. The child had grown and changed over the years, but the mother had not. Her tears were bitter. Her response to my question about why she was crying was, "I'm crying for myself."

Our Journey

The spiritual journey of parenthood happens when we take our daily cares, occasional ambivalence, and deepest joys to God. We can gain help and God's blessing when we structure our spiritual journey by using the discipline of *Lectio Divina*. By learning from God's parenting of characters in the Bible and from Jesus' relationship with his parents, by praying over Scripture and over our lives with our children, and finally, by taking the time to allow the two powerful tools of scriptural study and prayer to quietly rise in us like dough before baking, then we can gain insights that can help us grow spiritually. Spiritual growth during parenting not only makes us better parents to our children but prepares us for life after our children. As sad as the mother was who wept bitter tears at the end of her daughter's high school career, so too are those parents who come to the end of their children's childhood and can't wait for them to leave. There comes a time when young people ought to be on their own, but too often parents and children are sick of one another at the end of high school. That is a shame and it is unnecessary.

Parents who do not grow spiritually can grow out of their calling. Yes, the calling to parenthood can become moribund! Nothing in life is static; what doesn't grow, dies. By being open to God's insights to each new stage of parenting and to each new phase of a child's life, we can retain the richness and the joy of being a parent. We only lose our calling when we refuse to close each part of a child's life with a prayer of thanksgiving and we miss opening a new chapter with the optimism we had when we brought the newborn home. Parenting is a high calling we share with God Almighty. We can expect no more than the ups and downs our Creator experienced.

Despite the importance of being a good parent and the tragedies left behind by bad ones, parenting in our culture is still not honored as it deserves. Yet we who would be godly parents must not wish to be honored as kings, only to be found acceptable in the eyes of God.

An Unhistoric Act

Politicians talk a great deal about helping parents, but political schemes and government programs come and go while the task of rearing a child seems to become more difficult. What remains a fact is that being a parent is not sexy or professionally fulfilling. It really doesn't prepare you for much, other than grandparenthood! But being prepared to be a good grandparent can be very important. Here is some grandfatherly wisdom.

In the opening pages of *The Education of Henry Adams*, the autobiography of the early twentieth-century American historian Henry B. Adams, is one of my favorite stories about good grandparenting. Adams is the author who gave us a great deal to think about on the subject of the lasting effects of a good education.

The scene I remember comes from Adams' early childhood. It takes place in the home of his grandfather, the former President of the United States, John Quincy Adams. The six-year-old Henry is refusing to go to school, and his mother, embarrassed by the behavior of her son in her father-in-law's house, is about to give in, when suddenly the door of the library opens and the ex-President comes slowly down the stairs.

> Putting on his hat, he took the boy's hand without a word and walked with him, paralyzed by awe, up the road to the town. Henry was surprised when the eighty-year-old grandfather, instead of turning back under the hot morning sun, did not release the boy's hand until they had traveled the entire mile to the schoolhouse. Many years later, Adams humorously noted . . . receiving this first lesson in political philosophy.[7]

Notice that no rancor nor any ill will results from this exchange. In fact, quite the opposite is the lasting memory the child has of his grandfather. Notice also, as the recollection continues, that a crucial ingredient in the success of this event was the grandfather's use of silence. Children appreciate good examples and economy of words. Words used in the discipline of a child often convey anger and frustration disproportionate to the severity of the event. Who knows what the elderly President Adams may have been doing in his library, but he allowed none of the other events of his life to spill over into the discipline of the grandson. President Adams taught two lessons that day, for I suspect the boy's mother learned a good deal as well. Henry continues his reflections in the third-person on his grandfather's actions:

> The point was that this act, . . . ought to have made him dislike his grandfather for life. He could not recall that it had this effect even for a

moment. With a certain maturity of mind, the child must have recognized that the President, though a tool of tyranny, had done his disreputable work with a certain intelligence. He had shown no temper, no irritation, no personal feeling, and had made no display of force. Above all, he had held his tongue. During their long walk he said nothing; he had uttered no syllable of revolting cant about the duty of obedience and the wickedness of resistance to law; he had shown no concern in the matter; hardly even a consciousness of the boy's existence.[8]

We are not called to rear perfect children, nor are we expected never to make a mistake. We will be judged by God not by the things we have given to our children, nor even by what they do, but by what has fed their hearts and minds. What has been held up to them as good, and what has nourished their souls? We will be asked if what we gave our children were spiritual gifts that "neither moth nor rust consumes" and that "thieves do not break in and steal" (Matt. 6:20).

To give a child a spiritual inheritance of real substance requires vigilance and commitment. If we are unwilling to do the hard work of trying to shape them, we cannot bemoan the values of our children. I know a teacher who heard in a faculty meeting that a bright young girl was having difficulty in school mostly because of her chaotic home life. The atmosphere at home was dominated by two emotionally immature parents. The teacher took it upon herself, with the parents' permission, to take the girl home with her, to allow the girl to spend some evenings studying with her and her family, and to enjoy a typical family evening. The teacher simply wanted the girl to experience evenings when parents and children settled into a routine of an afterschool snack, followed by homework (while the teacher prepared for the next school day), and then dinner. There was no magic to the experiment, no lectures about organization. It was simply a wonderful teacher sharing her family's life with a lucky girl. In a short period of time, the girl began to understand how to create a more organized school night for herself. She eventually was able to help her parents as well. This teacher, like President Adams, chose the most powerful tool for the instruction: silent example.

Our children remember our actions, even if they don't seem to be listening to our words. During the funeral eulogy for a woman who had been a long-time friend and colleague of mine, the woman's son told a wonderful story. When he was a teenager, he experimented with sneaking out of the house to meet friends. He would leave after he was sure his parents were asleep. His parents grew suspicious of his behavior, and when they confronted him, he lied. The boy knew that his parents were early-to-bed and sound sleepers, and he assumed they would never catch on. The boy, now a father himself, said that his father seemed to accept his story, but his mother looked dubious. One night, as he crept back into the house in the wee hours of the morning, he was startled to find his mother asleep in his bed. When he entered the room his mother awoke, kissed him, and without a word went to her bedroom. The son said that he never came in late again, and his mother never mentioned the event. The mother's action didn't make the nightly news that night. She never became famous, except in her son's eyes.

George Eliot ends her nineteenth-century novel *Middlemarch* with a description of the heroine, Dorothea Brooke. What Eliot wrote of Dorothea can be said of all parents who work to give their children a spiritual inheritance:

> The effect of her being on those around her was incalculably diffusive: for the growing good of the world is partly dependent on unhistoric acts[9]

Or as the Bible puts it:

> "[I]n the Lord your labor is not in vain." (1 Cor. 15:58b)

Ten Things Parents Can Do
to Transform Parenting into a Spiritual Journey

1. Pray the Lord's Prayer every day. Before you pray, reflect on it from the perspective of your calling as a parent. Remember, Jesus was a son, and God was a parent. They will understand your prayer.

2. Remind yourself that you are the "baker" of a child, but not the maker. Children are God's gift, our job as a parent is to bring out the goodness within them. You are not responsible for what they choose to become, only for what they are exposed to as they are becoming.

3. Ask your children to forgive you when you are wrong and thank them for their forgiveness.

4. Be humble. You have been given the most important role in a human being's life, one that will touch him or her for a lifetime. Before you speak, before you act, reflect on the awesomeness of your role.

5. Face anger at your children when it comes and offer it up to God. When you give it to God, you won't give it to your child.

6. You will be humbled by your children no matter how hard you try. The good thing is, it happens to us all. Find some friends, perhaps a support group or discussion group sponsored by your church, and attend it regularly. It's good to have kindred spirits to talk to about your conflicting feelings. These thoughts will take flight when exposed.

7. Remind yourself that what you say to a child through your actions means more than your words. Be authentic.

8. Make sure your children have an older adult in their lives. Work hard at maintaining ties with grandparents. Remember, parents might pass on some emotional baggage to children, but grandparents rarely do. A wise, old ear can be a great release for a child.

9. Your children are not your monuments. It's O.K. if they are not like you.

10. Keep visible rainbows in your life, small reminders of the reasons you wanted children in the first place. Keep them out so you can see them on the days when you might forget.

NOTES

INTRODUCTION

1. Dana Mack, *The Assault on Parenthood: How Our Culture Undermines the Family* (New York: Simon & Schuster, 1997), 19.
2. The Reverend Janet Legro, parent seminar, St. Paul's Memorial Church, Charlottesville, Va., November 6, 1999.

CHAPTER ONE: THE COMPANIONSHIP OF GOD

1. CDC, 1999; Hoyert et al., 1999, as quoted in *Mental Health: A Report of the Surgeon General*, Chapter 3, 1999, <www.surgeongeneral.gov>.
2. Jack Canfield, Mark Victor Hansen, and Kimberly Kirberger, eds., *Chicken Soup for the Teenage Soul: 101 Stories of Life, Love, and Learning* (Deerfield Beach, Fla.: Health Communications, Inc., 1997), 55–6.
3. Alexander Dumas, *The Count of Monte Cristo* (New York: New American Library, 1988), 57.
4. Dale A. Matthews and Connie Clark, *The Faith Factor: Proof of the Healing Power of Prayer* (New York: Penguin Books, 1998), 137–8.
5. Elain Pagels, *The Origin of Satan* (New York: Vintage Books, 1995), 115–126.
6. Ramsay MacMullen, *Christianizing the Roman Empire (A.D. 100–400)* (New Haven, Conn.: Yale University Press, 1984), 30. "The only account given of the Carthaginian prison guard's change of heart as he observed the conduct of the group of his prisoners is: 'he began to make much of us, realizing there was a *virtus,* a miraculous power, in us until in the end the guard in the prison now believed.'"
7. Hebert Musurillo, *The Acts of the Christian Martyrs* (Oxford: Clarendon Press, 1972), 55, 59.
8. MacMullen, *Christianizing the Roman Empire*, 31.
9. Naomi H. Rosenblatt and Joshua Horwitz, *Wrestling with Angels: What Genesis Teaches Us about Our Spiritual Identity, Sexuality, and Personal Relationships* (New York: Dell Publishing, 1995), xix.
10. Gunnlaugur A. Jónsson, *The Image of God: Genesis 1:26–28 in a Century of Old Testament Research*, trans. Dr. Lorraine Svendsen (Stockholm: Almqvist & Wiksell International, 1988), 11.
11. Ibid., 12 ("image" [Greek = *imago*] and "likeness" [Greek = *similitudo*]).
12. It is important to note that Irenaeus was one of the first in the church to see the Old

and New Testaments (although he did not use these terms) as composing the full revelation of God's message. He resisted the notion, popular amongst the gnostic teachers of his day, that the Hebrew Bible was a collection of superstitions unrelated to Jesus' "spiritual" message. Much of his work attempted to reconcile the Old and New Testament teachings (including the plural reference to God in Genesis) with the teachings of Jesus.

13. Karl Barth, *Church Dogmatics*, III/1, ed. Rev. Prof. G. W. Bromiley and Rev. Prof. T. F. Torrance, trans. Rev. Harold Knight, Rev. Prof. G. W. Bromiley, Rev. Prof. J. K. S. Reid, and Rev. Prof. R. H. Fuller (Edinburgh: T. & T. Clark, 1960), 192.

14. Shirley C. Guthrie, *Christian Doctrine*, rev. ed. (Louisville, Ky.: Westminster John Knox Press, 1994), 75.

15. Barth's discussion is in a fifteen and one-half page footnote on Genesis 1:26 in his massive *Church Dogmatics*. His disquisition bears a striking resemblance, in the mind of this author, to the work of Martin Buber in his 1923 book, *I and Thou*; Martin Buber, *I and Thou* (New York: Charles Scribner's Sons, 1970).

16. Barth, *Church Dogmatics*, 196.

17. Rosenblatt, *Wrestling with Angels*, xx.

CHAPTER TWO: FINDING GOD

1. C. S. Lewis, *Mere Christianity* (New York: Simon & Schuster, 1996), 11.

2. John Oxenham, "In Christ There Is No East or West," in *The Presbyterian Hymnal*, ed. LindaJo McKim (Louisville, Ky.: Westminster/John Knox Press, 1990), no. 440.

3. Martin Luther, "Nativity," in *Martin Luther's Christmas Book*, ed. Ronald Bainton (Minneapolis: Augsburg Fortress Publishers, 1997), 31.

4. Luke 9:59ff., Matthew 8:21ff.

5. Erik H. Erikson, *Childhood and Society* (New York: W. W. Norton & Co., Inc., 1950, 2d ed., 1963) 262.

6. Diogenes Allen, *Spiritual Theology: The Theology of Yesterday for Spiritual Help Today* (Boston: Cowley Publications, 1997), 48.

7. Roger Rosenblatt, *Coming Apart: A Memoir of the Harvard Wars of 1969* (Boston: Little, Brown & Company, 1997).

CHAPTER THREE: A TRANSCENDENT PERSPECTIVE

1. Vaclav Havel, "A Sense of the Transcendent," *Cross Currents: The Journal of the Association for Religion and Intellectual Life* 47 (Fall 1997): 298.

2. Thomas Fitzgerald, "The Future of Belief," *First Things* 63 (May 1996): 23–27.

3. Romans 4:3, James 2:23.

4. John Calvin, *Commentaries*, vol. I, trans. The Rev. John King, M.A. (Grand Rapids, Mich.: Baker Book House, 1996), 563.

5. November 18, 1978.

6. Isaiah 41:8: "But you, Israel, my servant, Jacob, whom I have chosen, the offspring of Abraham, my friend." James 2:23: "Thus the Scripture was fulfilled that says, 'Abraham believed God, and it was reckoned to him as righteousness,' and he was called the friend of God."

7. Samuel J. Schultz, *The Old Testament Speaks*, 3d ed. (San Fransisco: Harper and Row, 1980), 34.

8. Sarah was Abraham's half-sister as well as his wife, a point later clarified in Scripture: Genesis 20:12.

9. Genesis 13:8.

10. Gary Anderson, "Introduction to Israelite Religion," *The New Interpreter's Bible*, vol.1, ed. David L. Petersen (Nashville: Abingdon Press, 1994), 280.

11. Edward Norbeck, *Religion in Primitive Society* (New York: Harper & Row, 1961), 65.

12. Martin Luther, *Luther's Works*, ed. Jaroslav Pelikan, vol. 3 (St. Louis: Concordia Publishing House, 1961), 21.

13. Richard Elliott Friedman, *The Disappearance of God: A Divine Mystery* (Boston: Little, Brown & Co., 1995). Note the book was re-released as *The Hidden Face of God*.

14. Ibid., 7.

15. Ibid., 14.

16. Ibid., 17.

17. Ibid., 20. Note, Friedman adds that the sole possible exception to this statement is "The Lord spoke to Manasseh and all his people" (2 Chr. 33:10). The text notes, "But they gave no heed."

18. Ibid., 129.

19. Ralph C. Wood, "In Defense of Disbelief," *First Things* 86 (Oct. 1998): 32.

20. You might be surprised to learn that fourth-century desert monks could write insightfully about human relationships. Although these early monastics usually lived in separate compartments, they came together as a community for certain activities like worship, study, and common meals. The work of one of these Desert Fathers speaks to a particularly pressing issue we face as parents: His name was Evagrius. Evagrius was one of the most prolific writers of all the Desert Fathers, and his writings were well known in his day throughout Christendom. A frequent topic of his work was what we might call the "family dynamics" of monks. As in any family or community, competing interests, distractions, and unproductive disagreements often fueled controversy and mitigated the positive dynamic within the group.

Evagrius didn't start in the desert. Before he chose to live a life of self-imposed isolation, Evagrius was the chief advisor to St. Gregory of Nazianzus in the heated battle over the Nicene Creed that took place during the fourth century in Constantinople. Evagrius played an important role in the ultimate acceptance of the Nicene Creed as one of the earliest and fullest expressions of orthodox Christian faith.

We may not attach either Gregory's name or Evagrius' to the Nicene Creed. In fact, if most people have heard of either it is Gregory, for he is well known in literature for his list of the Seven Deadly Sins. These are the acts that separate us from God and lead us to the death of the soul. The deadly sins are pride, covetousness, lust, anger, gluttony, envy, and sloth.

Evagrius' contribution to Gregory's thinking on this matter is not known, but we do know that Evagrius had earlier published his own list, which he called the Deadly Thoughts. His list numbered eight and included an additional failing to worry about: "vainglory."

21. Ponticus Evagrius, *Praktikos & On Prayer*, trans. Simon Tugwell (London: Oxford Press, 1987), 28.

22. John Bunyan, *The Pilgrim's Progress from This World to That Which Is to Come; Delivered under the Similtude of a Dream* (Auburn: Derby and Miller. Buffalo: Geo. H. Derby and Co. 1853), part 1, seventh stage, <www.ccel.org/b/bunyan/progress/pilgrim-all.txt>.

Now, a little before it was day, good Christian, as one half amazed, brake out into this passionate speech: What a fool, quoth he, am I, thus to lie in a stinking dungeon, when I may as well walk at liberty! I have a key in my bosom, called Promise, that will, I am persuaded, open any lock in Doubting Castle. Then said Hopeful, That is good news; good brother, pluck it out of thy bosom, and try.

Then Christian pulled it out of his bosom, and began to try at the dungeon-door, whose bolt, as he turned the key, gave back, and the door flew open with ease, and Christian and Hopeful both came out. Then he went to the outward door that leads into the castle-yard, and with his key opened that door also. After he went to the iron gate, for that must be opened too; but that lock went desperately hard, yet the key did open it. They then thrust open the gate to make their escape with speed; but that gate, as it opened, made such a creaking, that it waked Giant Despair, who hastily rising to pursue his prisoners, felt his limbs to fail, for his fits took him again, so that he could by no means go after them. Then they went on, and came to the King's highway, and so were safe, because they were out of his jurisdiction.

23. M. Scott Peck, *The Road Less Traveled: A New Psychology of Love, Traditional Values and Spiritual Growth* (New York: Simon & Schuster, 1978), 17.

CHAPTER FOUR: TRUTH: THE ABSOLUTE HORIZON

1. Bill Moyers, *Genesis: A Living Conversation* (New York: Doubleday, 1996), 44.

CHAPTER FIVE: THE FREEDOM TO DOUBT

1. 1 Corinthians 9:24; Hebrews 12:1.

2. Havel, "A Sense of the Transcendent," 298.

3. "Episcopal, Congregational, Presbyterian, Methodist, and Disciples of Christ suffered a net membership loss of 5.2 million people during the years [1964–1985] when the U.S. population rose by 47 million." Quoted in Jack Rogers, *Claiming the Center: Churches and Conflicting Worldviews* (Louisville, Ky.: Westminster John Knox Press, 1995), 24.

4. Ibid., 6.

5. Allan Bloom, *The Closing of the American Mind: How Higher Education Has Failed Democracy and Impoverished the Souls of Today's Students* (New York: Simon & Schuster, 1987), 25.

6. Ibid., 50.

7. Stephen L. Carter, *The Culture of Disbelief: How American Law and Politics Trivialize Religious Devotion* (New York: Doubleday, 1993) 217.

8. The philosophy of James was moderate compared to the "radical pragmatism" of John Dewey, the most influential figure in the development of American public education. Of Dewey, James once wrote that he and Dewey "absolutely agree."

9. William James, *The Varieties of Religious Experience* (New York: Penguin Books, 1982), 144.

10. Ibid., 144.

11. Letter from Thomas Jefferson to Dupont de Nemours, April 24, 1816.

12. Peter Berger, "At Stake in the Enlightenment," *First Things* 61 (March 1996): 13–19.

13. Carter, *Culture of Disbelief*, 226 (quoting historian Robert Nesbit).

14. John Dewey, *The Quest for Certainty: A Study of the Relation of Knowledge and Action* (New York: Minton, Balch & Company, 1929), 72.

15. Carter, *Culture of Disbelief*, 173.

16. *A Nation at Risk: The Imperative for Educational Reform*, A Report to the Nation and the Secretary of Education, U. S. Department of Education by the National Commission on Excellence in Education, April 1983.

17. Jean-Jacques Rousseau, *Emile*, trans. Allan Bloom (U.S.A.: Basic Books, Inc., 1979), 67.

18. Ibid., 8.

19. Ibid., 15.

20. Diogenes Allen, *Christian Belief in a Postmodern World: The Full Wealth of Conviction* (Louisville, Ky.: Westminster/John Knox Press, 1989), 2.

21. Berger, "At Stake in the Enlightenment," 13–19.

22. James Davison Hunter, *Culture Wars: The Struggle to Define America* (New York: Basic Books, 1991).

23. Everett Mendelsohn, "Religious Fundamentalism and the Sciences," *Fundamentalisms and Society: Reclaiming the Sciences, the Family, and Education*, vol. 2, ed. Martin E. Marty and R. Scott Appleby (Chicago: The University of Chicago Press, 1993), 25.

24. Emmanuel Sivan, "The Enclave Culture," *Fundamentalisms Comprehended*, vol. 5, ed. Martin E. Marty and R. Scott Appleby (Chicago: University of Chicago Press, 1995), 27.

25. Ibid., 18.

26. Robert H. Bork, *Slouching Towards Gomorrah: Modern Liberalism and American Decline* (New York: Regan Books, 1996), 250ff.

27. St. Benedict, *The Holy Rule of St. Benedict*, trans. Rev. Boniface Verheyen (1949) chapter III.

28. Wood, "In Defense of Disbelief," 28.

29. *The Interpreter's Bible*, vol. 9 (New York/Nashville: Abingdon Press, 1954), 229.

30. Wood, "In Defense of Disbelief," 28.

CHAPTER SIX: HONOR

1. Matthew 3:1ff, Mark 1:12ff, and Luke 4:1ff.

2. Edward A. Dowey Jr., *The Knowledge of God in Calvin's Theology* (New York: Columbia University Press, 1952), 37.

3. *The Westminster Confession of Faith, The Constitution of the Presbyterian Church (U.S.A.)*, Part 1, *Book of Confessions* (Louisville, Ky.: Office of the General Assembly, Presbyterian Church (U.S.A.), 1999), 6.009.

4. Janet Martin Soskice, *Metaphor and Religious Language* (Oxford: Clarendon Press, 1985), 159.

5. *Grimm's Complete Fairy Tales* (New York: Barnes & Nobles, Inc., 1993), 362.

6. Peck, *The Road Less Traveled*, 21.

7. John 17:24.

8. Bernhard W. Anderson, *Understanding the Old Testament*, 2d ed. (Englewood Cliffs, N.J.: Prentice-Hall, Inc., 1966), 320.

9. Ibid., 293.

10. Walter Brueggemann, *Genesis, Interpretation: A Bible Commentary for Teaching and Preaching*, ed. James Luther Mays, vol. 1 (Atlanta: John Knox Press, 1982), 57.

11. Gunther Plaut, "Genesis 4:1–16: Cain and Abel: Bible, Tradition, and Contemporary Reflection," *Preaching Biblical Texts: Expositions by Jewish and Christian Scholars*, ed. Fredrick C. Holmgren and Herman E. Schaalman (Grand Rapids, Mich.: William B. Eerdmans Publishing Company, 1995), 12. Thanks to Rabbi Gunther Plaut for this observation.
12. Genesis 19:30–38.
13. Reported on CNN, October 22, 1998 during the Clinton peace talks in Maryland.

CHAPTER SEVEN: THE TRIUMPH OF *TIMSHEL*

1. Martin Luther King Jr., "Love, Law and Civil Disobedience," *A Testament of Hope: The Essential Writings of Martin Luther King, Jr.*, ed. Coretta Scott King (New York: Harper & Row, 1986), 48.
2. Ibid., 48.
3. Scott Peck reflects the state of modern psychology's struggle to understand the concept of evil. He writes, "evil is laziness . . . , love is the antithesis of laziness" (Peck, *The Road Less Traveled*, 278). Our modern world often prefers evil to be the result of madness. But one thing we all learned from the terrorist attacks on the World Trade Center and the Pentagon is that terrorists are evil, but they are not crazy.
4. Guthrie, *Christian Doctrine*, 221.
5. Pagels, *Origin of Satan*, 39.
6. Ibid., 34.
7. Ibid., 39.
8. Ibid., 180.
9. John Steinbeck, *East of Eden* (New York: Penguin Books, 1952), 398–9.
10. Brueggeman, *Genesis*, 57.
11. Numbers 21:9.
12. B. A. Gerrish, *The Old Protestantism and the New: Essays on the Reformation Heritage* (Edinburgh: T. & T. Clark, 1982), 57.
13. Judges 4:21.

CHAPTER EIGHT: THE SPIRITUAL JOURNEY OF PARENTHOOD

1. David Elkind, *The Hurried Child: Growing Up Too Fast Too Soon* (Reading, Mass.: Addison-Wesley Publishing Co., 1981).
2. Luigi Pirandello, "War," *21 Great Stories*, ed. Abraham H. Lass and Norma L. Tasman (New York: Penguin Group, 1969), 14.
3. Jack Miles, *God: A Biography* (New York: Vintage Books, 1996), 67.
4. Allen, *Spiritual Theology*, 86.
5. Middle English *deliveren*, from Old French *delivrer*, from Late Latin *dêlìberâre*: Latin *dê-, de-* + *lìberâre*, to free (from *lìber*, free).
6. Pagels, *Origin of Satan*, 39.
7. Henry Adams, *The Education of Henry Adams* (New York: Modern Library, 1934), 13, as quoted in John Patrick Diggins, *The Promise of Pragmatism* (Chicago: The University of Chicago Press, 1994), 55–6.
8. Ibid., 55–6.
9. George Eliot, *Middlemarch* (Harmondsworth, Middlesex: Penguin Books Ltd., 1871–1872), 896.

INDEX OF SCRIPTURE

INDEX OF SUBJECTS